DUNKLIN COUNTY MISSOURI MARRIAGE RECORDS

Volume 2, 1916-1927

Transcribed and Compiled by
Linda L. Green

WILLOW BEND BOOKS
2005

WILLOW BEND BOOKS
AN IMPRINT OF HERITAGE BOOKS, INC.

Books, CDs, and more – Worldwide

For our listing of thousands of titles see our website
at
www.HeritageBooks.com

Published 2005 by
HERITAGE BOOKS, INC.
Publishing Division
65 East Main Street
Westminster, Maryland 21157-5026

International Standard Book Number: **0-7884-3164-1**

Introduction

Marriage records of many Missouri counties have not been transcribed and/or published. The Archives is full of information just waiting for people to transcribe it to make it available to others.

When the folks in Salt Lake City, Utah, microfilmed these marriage records they did the best they could, and this was the best grouping of records I've transcribed so far. Microfilm available for sale is therefore third or even fourth generation and becomes more faint as more copies are made from the originals provided to the State Archives or Missouri State Historical Society.

Sometimes, either the bride or groom was legible but not the other or maybe just a first name of one or the other. Hopefully at least one name was complete.

This volume comprises the dates 1916-1927. There is not a complete index at the back of the book, but an index after each volume. This should make it easier for people to look up the records.

Linda L. Green
13950 Ruler Court
Woodbridge, VA 22193

Table of Contents

Volume 13 1916-1919

Though there are very few records for colored marriages in Dunklin County, the use of col for colored does show up a few times.

GROOM	BRIDE	SOLEMNIZED
A. L. Sikes	Sciola Hicks	8 Dec 1916
A. A. Huffman	Mrs. Elizabeth Brewer	8 Dec 1916
E.A. Presley	Minnie Johnson	10 Dec 1916
John W. Holmes	Ersie James	11 Dec 1916
C. M. Webb	Nora Bighan	11 Dec 1916
C. E. Potts	K. Downing	4 Dec 1916
Burch Blakemore	Leota Green	3 Dec 1916
Langdon R. Jones	Mode Benson	22 Dec 1916
Clifford Butler	Rhoda Daughten	13 Dec 1916
Ben Ashworth	Gladys Irene Collins	14 Dec 1916
Henry Hand	Emma McKinney	17 Dec 1916
Luther Austin	May Stonum	18 Dec 1916
J. W. McAlexander	Mrs. A. G. Clayton	6 Dec 1916
G. T. Johnson	Niece McKinney	3 Dec 1916
J. R. Oliver	Maggie Monehan	20 Dec 1916
Elmer T. Acord	Irene Cantrell	10 Dec 1916
G. T. Lawless	Iva Stricklin	18 Dec 1916
Will Boyd	Minnie May Jones	12 Dec 1916
Leonard C. Arnold	Sylvia Marie Gregory	16 Dec 1916
J. C. Gordon	Cora Earnest	16 Dec 1916
Homer Perkins	Mary Ray	13 Dec 1916
Levi Healy	Mrs. Francis Lay	13 Dec 1916
Jonie F. Cook	Bertha Baugher	22 Dec 1916
J. R. Malady	Thelyann Singleton	17 Dec 1916
Bert Griffin	Mammie Bitticks	16 Dec 1916
Loid Butler	Ethel Skidmore	24 Dec 1916
E. S. Skidmore	Effie Smothers	24 Dec 1916
Bernie Underwood	Ruth Nixon	23 Dec 1916
W. J. Sexton	Ethel Smith	24 Dec 1916
Lawrence Smithwick	Rosie Wilkins	20 Dec 1916
Bryant Heathcutt	Mrs. Minnie Rupple	22 Dec 1916
C. H. Linn	Martha Huggins	25 Dec 1916
Icom Grimsley	Sarah Perkins	23 Dec 1916
Elbert Harty	Gertha Provance	24 Dec 1916
Roger White	Edith Collias	23 Dec 1916

GROOM	BRIDE	SOLEMNIZED
Oscar Elgland	Lettie Fletcher	23 Dec 1916
H. A. Kirby	Retta Campbell	26 Dec 1916
J. W. Claxton	Bessie Prue	26 Dec 1916
Robert Hughes	Laura Parsons	23 Dec 1916
Pete Maberry	Hazel Stumps	27 Dec 1916
C. F. Davenport	Connie Elmore	28 Dec 1916
Richard Walls	Allie Slayton	28 Dec 1916
Albert Bridges	Florence Johnson	6 Dec 1916
Walter Rauls	Ruth Rauls	27 Dec 1916
John Snaveley	Neeley Kent	28 Dec 1916
Irwin Carrell	Voda Drope	29 Dec 1916
Fred Allen	Beulah McGruder	11 Jan 1917
Elmer Studdard	Emma Dowdy	15 Dec 1916
F. H. Tyler	Mrs. Ahrnie L. Tyler	24 Dec 1916
Frank Vase	Syntha B. Allen	26 Dec 1916
Matthew Middaugh	Mrs. Cora McNew	6 Jan 1917
Albert Lester	Alma Eaker	31 Dec 1916
T. H. Bridges	Mrs. Belle Matthews	8 Jan 1917
George Welch	Martha Overturf	9 Jan 1917
Tommie Moore	Vander Myer	6 Jan 1917
Lanie Irby	Rosy Shipley	9 Jan 1917
Harvey Diggs	Lucy Walls	6 Jan 1917
J. D. Harmon	Pearl Young	7 Jan 1917
J. G. Kiltbreath	Della Woods	11 Jan 1917
M. D. Ladd	Drusill Smith	10 Jan 1917
Frank O'Gwyn	Ruth Ward	30 Nov 1916
J. D. Doherty	Grace Irene Rose	28 Nov 1916
Chas. Thompson	Myrtle Harper	10 Jan 1917
B. M. Craig	Mrs. Jennie Lacy	23 Dec 1916
Floyd House	Essie James	10 Jan 1917
W. T. Bassett	Isalee McKinnis	13 Jan 1917
A. A. Shrum	Flossie Hartsoe	16 Jan 1917
Robert H. Douglass	Hilda Rebecca Blakemore	7 Jan 1917
J. P. Collins	Mrs. Ina Hollifield	16 Jan 1917
J. F. McAuliffe	Pearl M. Burlison	18 Jan 1917
Earl Sutton	Beulah Starnes	18 Jan 1917
Athel Mangold	Pearl Dye	20 Jan 1917
Curray Williams	Minnie Davis	18 Jan 1917
A. H. Rast	Mrs. Jennie Roat	10 Jan 1917
Oscar C. Fry	Lillie F. Stewart	9 Jan 1917
J. H. Anthony	Mrs. Eva Duke	21 Jan 1917
D. F. Ferrell	Clara Neighbors	21 Jan 1917
Harrison Davis	Clara Williams	4 Feb 1917
Elbert Horner	Julia Shook	13 Jan 1917

GROOM	BRIDE	SOLEMNIZED
Frank Morgan	Hester Simpson	28 Jan 1917
Tony H. Stelle	Elizabeth F. Stenger	24 Jan 1917
Crulius Marshall	Lucy Baker	24 Jan 1917
J. B. Ford	Mary Thacker	24 Jan 1917
G.H. Brush	Mrs. W. A. Cutler	Date Not Shown
Ira L. Hampton	Ollie M. Reagan	24 Jan 1917
John W. Smith	Florence Coble	24 Jan 1917
R. C. Johnson	Mrs. Cora Willoughby	Date Not Shown
G. W. Smithson	Carrie Thacker	23 Jan 1917
Charly Davis	Pearl Davis	31 Jan 1917
Grover Runnels	Tressie Faughen	1 Feb 1917
S. A. Ray	Mrs. S. M. Glenny	12 Feb 1917
T. M Carnal	Mrs. M. J. Vanthaugh	12 Feb 1917
Jim Batchelor	Elsie Sullivan	21 Feb 1917
Lee Keown	Mrs. Sarah Moore	17 Feb 1917
C. R. Davis	Ruby Eudaly	7 Oct 1916
Charles S. Bowden	Bessie Lowe	8 Feb 1917
Chas. T. Williamson	Tommie Elder	18 Feb 1917
Glen Sercy	Rosa Allen	18 Feb 1917
Percy H. Barbee	Edna Hollister	Feb 1917
Thomas Sandefer	Delma James	12 Feb 1917
H. B. Kelley	Vera Gruggett	9 Feb 1917
James Higginbotham	Nora Cato	20 Feb 1917
J. W. Ingram	Jannie Lane	21 Feb 1917
Zalmer C. Butler	Callie Wilkins	26 Jan 1917
Alphonse Maples	Daisy Cagle	19 Feb 1917
Will Shawn	Ruth Baker	24 Feb 1917
James R. Johnson	Bertha Goldsmith	22 Feb 1917
Thed Renard	Velma Wilson	25 Feb 1917
Oscar Small	Christine Renfrow	26 Feb 1917
King James Boozer	Rose V. Wayne	25 Feb 1917
Obediah Dye	Sulla Arnold	25 Feb 1917
Albert Horner	Dorris Zachery	24 Feb 1917
Marion Clark	Mrs. Mable Dickson	24 Feb 1917
Truman Jaques	Flora Welker	24 Feb 1917
W. E. Daniels	Hester P. Dunscomb	28 Feb 1917
C. Hubbard	Amanda Garvins	27 Feb 1917
Pinkney Acuff	Delphia Mills	28 Feb 1917
W. H. Southern	Bessie Massey	1 Mar 1917
Elmer Jones	Kitty May Hull	2 Mar 1917
Alva Hart	Maude Busby	3 Mar 1917
G. A. Douglass	Maude Luckett	4 Mar 1917
Bill Harmon	Iva Young	5 Mar 1917
L. C. Hinesley	Martha Brooks	7 Mar 1917

GROOM	BRIDE	SOLEMNIZED
Clarence Turner	Mrs. Mary McPherson	6 Mar 1917
Arthur Shelton	Bertha Sheehy	7 Mar 1917
A. F. Wells	Mrs. Ida Grogan	8 Mar 1917
Roy Stark	Louisa Huffman	12 Apr 1917
J. F. McHaney	Annie L. Barham	12 Feb 1917
E. L. Kinsey	Annie Teel	21 Feb 1917
G. W. Carter	Susie Moss	10 Mar 1917
S. H. Buck	Betheny Langston	Mar 1917
Emmitt Sutton	Beatrice T. Reeves	16 Mar 1917
Frank Holland	Elsie M. Sims	19 Mar 1917
John Tate	Mamie Ezell	15 Mar 1917
Alvin Bishop	Louise Wilson	18 Mar 1917
A. M. Boyd	Bessie Davis	20 Mar 1917
Lawrence Slinkard	Perlie Childs	18 Mar 1917
James A. Beggs	Mrs. Lizzie Summers	21 Mar 1917
Chas. E. Wilkins	Joe Annie Nelson	17 Mar 1917
A. W. York	Mrs. Maude Sturges	18 Mar 1917
Bert Ramsey	Lillie Meyers	28 Mar 1917
E. P. Duncan	Mirttie Russell	2 Feb 1917
Martin L. Crites	Stella Wilburn	24 Mar 1917
Geo. W. Baker	Mary O'Brien	26 Mar 1917
L. S. Brown	Mrs. Martha E. Lackler (Lackles)	25 Mar 1911 (1917)
Van Smedley	Ada Cude	7 Mar 1917
Earl Mabry	Luby Evans	19 Mar 1917
Ollie R. Barah	Josie Moore	24 Mar 1917
Clyde Greenfield	Mrs. Edna Keaton	31 Mar 1917
Mat Stockinger	Lucy V. Frederick	31 Mar 1917
George Napper	Nadine Patterson	7 Feb 1917
Albert Daves	Mary Perry	30 Mar 1917
Henry Neal	Willa Paskel	1 Apr 1917
J.J. Heere (Heese)	Nellie Davis	29 Mar 1917
Jake Pendell	Faye Burnett	4 Mar 1917
Albert Pennington	Mrs. Ader Anders	5 Apr 1917
Will Bell	Mrs. Elsie Belle	5 Apr 1917
I. B. Minner	Pherebe Delaney Pendleton	5 Apr 1917
Johny Jones	Mattie Green	2 Apr 1917
Howard Vaughn	Hallie Brown	30 Mar 1917
Frank Neighbors	Myrtle Carnes	7 Apr 1917
E. E. Burton	Jennie Shrum	6 Apr 1917
Odes Godwin	Vada Vaughn	8 Apr 1917
J. R. White	Mrs. M. A. Christian	12 Apr 1917
John A. Worthington	Jenning Northington	11 Apr 1917
Alva Hapwood	Virgia Harlin	15 Apr 1917
Lee McKinis	Stella Porter	14 Apr 1917

GROOM	BRIDE	SOLEMNIZED
Elmer Dennis	Hassie Ham	19 Apr 1917
Marcus McKay	Cora Hays	1 Apr 1917
Fred Rushin	Nora Milstead	22 Apr 1917
J. H. Rawls	Lemma Moody	21 Apr 1917
Charly M. Pounds	Mrs. Vara Dockens	24 Apr 1917
Martin Nichols Meiner	Willia Agatha Ward	25 Apr 1917
Walter Temple	Beatrice Weaver	17 Apr 1917
Andrew Jones	Mrs. Alice Pelts	28 Apr 1917
Virgil M. Miller	Vera Viola Grigory	29 Apr 1917
Rafford Bailey	Junia Byrd	April 1917
Will Jones	Eva Vanbiber	3 May 1917
Harry W. Masterman	Mrs. Nettie Nowell	6 May 1917
Robert Mizell	Lysie Elder	5 May 1917
Andrew C. Richardson	Mrs. Lizzie Revolon	6 May 1917
John C. McHaney	Ruby Irene Gettis	6 May 1917
Silas Spicer	Maggie Hilderbrand	9 May 1917
Alvin Williams	Millie Pipkins	8 May 1917
M. J. Skidmore	Pearl George	8 May 1917
Earl Leggett	Willna Taylor	8 May 1917
John Osborne	Mrs. Lillie Hurd	10 May 1917
Glenn Thomas	Anna Puckett	13 May 1917
J. T. Duggins	Mrs. Nora Robison	6 May 1917
Clyde Flake	Mrs. Hazel Northam	16 May 1917
J. E. Thrasher	Minnie Furgerson	12 May 1917
Vander Simpkins	Virginia Turner	17 May 1917
Clarence Hicks	Mrs. Grace Sutton	19 May 1917
Elijah N. Despain	Lillie Lutes	19 May 1917
Ed Turner	Bertha McDaniel	20 May 1917
Harry Hancock	Susie Vandine	20 May 1917
Virgil McClure	Onie Hafford	21 May 1917
Will Linton	Myrtle Perkins	21 May 1917
John N. Chislan	Laura DeHart	24 May 1917
A. F. Rose	Edith L. Conrad	21 May 1917
Emery Caldwell	Mrs. Ida Autrey	19 May 1917
J. P. Venters	Mrs. M. E. Thompson	26 May 1917
H. V. Vincent	Mary E. Douglass	30 May 1917
Harry Glenn Shackets	Edyth M. Post	30 May 1917
E. M. Forde	Ellie Telty	31 May 1917
B. C. Clayton	Enah Bane	27 May 1917
Robert Little	Opal Wright	26 May 1917
John Brewer	Hattie Stine	3 Jun 1917
I. W. Nance	Pearl Hutcheson	3 Jun 1917
Arthur Holtzhauser	Effie Alsup	3 Jun 1917
J. R. Merideth	Carrie Wemberly	4 Jun 1917

GROOM	BRIDE	SOLEMNIZED
Clarence Baker	Clara Grey	3 Jun 1917
Chas. N. Coburn	Maude E. Statler	7 Jun 1917
George Dicland	Florence Gravens	23 Jun 1917
Charles V. Hunter	Marian Irene Dunmire	4 Jun 1917
Rolla Sumner	Nettie East	7 Jun 1917
W. R. Drew	Mrs. Ada Parsons	11 Jun 1917
Lloyd Craig	Myrtle Allen	3 Jun 1917
J. A. Yates	Lanie Powell	28 Dec 1916
L. C. Sutton	Ora Bailey	11 Jun 1917
Burrel Harrison	Zadie Collins	10 Jun 1917
B. F. Akins	Edith Williamson	10 Jun 1917
J. M. Hammonds	Ola Thomas	8 Jun 1917
Raymond Parchman	Gracie Evern	8 Jun 1917
J. L. Watson	Francis Vail	10 Jun 1917
D. H. Slankard	Maggie Scott	8 Jun 1917
Robert Smalley	Rosey McNeil	3 Jun 1917
C. Jaker	M. M. Lynn	2 Jun 1917
Charly Adkins	Sarah Crabtree	12 Jun 1917
Otto Fletcher	Nora Sackman (Jackman)	13 Jun 1917
Robert Cherry	Ollie Henry	15 Jun 1917
Charles Teel	R. Zarney Ray	12 Jun 1917
Luther M. Petty	Mrs. Ola Arnold	18 Jun 1917
John F. Killen	Esther Fleeman	20 Jun 1917
James Warren	Mrs. Maude Deware	22 Jun 1917
Marion B. Jones	Laura Simmons	23 Jun 1917
Harve Mangoldew	Ethel Wilson	23 Jun 1917
J. C. Wheatley	Mamie Driskill	25 Jun 1917
Henry Cunningham	Mrs. Lillian Stanford	28 Jun 1917
Pete Mitchem	Eida Roberson	23 Jun 1917
W. A. Conder	Mrs. Lottie Fry	23 Jun 1917
James Barron	Grace Morse	25 Jun 1917
Joseph Campbell	Beulah Howard	29 Jun 1917
Willie Owens	Effie Acord	15 Jun 1917
Thomas Scott	Maggie Leech	30 Jun 1917
Ray Zackery	Georgia North	1 Jul 1917
N. C. Holt	Letha Hart	30 Jun 1917
Herman Hart	Louie Edwards	30 Jun 1917
W. C. Brigman	Beatrice Cobb	1 Jul 1917
F. W. Johnson	Pearl Lasater	2 Jul 1917
G. L. Mezoe	Birdie Eppihimer	1 Jun 1917
Will Rende	Stella Williams	4 Jul 1917
A. L. Gardner	Mrs. M. J. Jones	3 Jul 1917
Willis Brooks	Neoma Krapf	4 Jul 1917
Cullen Vanover	Grace McKinzie	4 Jul 1917

GROOM	BRIDE	SOLEMNIZED
L. M. Walter	Myrl Wegener	3 Jul 1917
C. L. Pelts	Lillie Sanders	3 Jul 1917
J. E. Noisworthy	Mrs. Lou Morris	4 Jul 1917
Earnest Fisher	Mrs. Georgia Athelton	7 Jul 1917
Sidney A. Sparks	Zola Belle Evans	4 Jul 1917
Ogle Lee Pippins	Mrs. Pearl Smith	24 Jun 1917
B. K. Kersey	Mrs. Anna Lane	26 Jun 1917
Bert Williamson	Eula Pool	1 Jul 1917
B. F. Garrett	Mrs. Iona Floy Greer	7 Jul 1917
Ira Ralph Bostwick	Lucile Dunivan	7 Jul 1917
Homer Waldon	Adella Hughes	12 Jul 1917
James Wesley Wicker	Vennie Watson	3 Jul 1917
Earle Borah	Nellie Bryant	26 May 1917
A. J. Moore	Tinnie Grimsley	14 Jul 1917
Johnie Starks (Stacks)	Nettie Bailey	16 Jul 1917
B. F Welty	Ruth Randol	8 Jul 1917
E. L. Launius	Delia Gorden	20 Jul 1917
James Kennedy	Anna Allen	21 Jul 1917
Henry Behr	Mary Taylor	18 Jul 1917
Leo John Ninier	Bertha May Pitts	26 Jul 1917
Ottie R. Ross	Flora E. Stafford	25 Jul 1917
I. B. Griffin	Ellen Crockett	26 Jul 1917
Robert L. Davis	Mrs. Clara Skeif	28 Jul 1917
Sid Bell	Gertie Little	22 Jul 1917
Benjamin F. Arnold	Alma Eva Eden	22 Jul 1917
Altha Gray	Flora Fortner	19 Jul 1917
Jake Alberson	Mrs. Lucy Moore	4 Aug 1917
G. E. Brunt	Anner Long	1 Aug 1917
W. M. Cato	Hazel Lovejoy	4 Aug 1917
L. R. Chapman	Delia Sitz	9 Aug 1917
J. A. Miller	Lena Crews	4 Aug 1917
L. E. Tate	Mrs. Nancy May	4 Aug 1917
Joseph B. Arr (Orr)	Marguerette Mofield	29 Jul 1917
Samuel B. King	Mabel Lee Jackson	15 Aug 1917
J. T. Hall	Mrs. Annie Harden	5 Aug 1917
Earl F. Pollock	Katie N. Baker	1 Jul 1917
John F. Winn	Dara C. Maples	20 Jul 1917
Alcine White	Ollie Ellington	8 Aug 1917
Jason Hampton	Mrs. Maggie Oller	4 Aug 1917
George Riley	Bertha Usrey	11 Aug 1917
Bob Patterson	Mrs. Opal Wallace	4 Aug 1917
W. M. Burr	Mrs. J. P. Howard	12 Aug 1917
Joseph N. Nelson	Mrs. Mollie Gray	13 Aug 1917
Ira George	Mrs. Fannie Deck	15 Aug 1917

GROOM	BRIDE	SOLEMNIZED
John Mounce	Sarah Dunn	25 Jul 1917
Edward N. Coleman	Mary Campbell	13 Jul 1917
Isaac Johnson	Mattie Kalish	16 Aug 1917
Dave Childers	Ida Cutler	16 Aug 1917
Johny Gales	Carrie B. Denis	23 Aug 1917
Ogle H. Hickerson	Florence N. Arnold	19 Aug 1917
Earnest H. Hoxworth	Orna Skief	15 Aug 1917
Troy E. Slinkard	Drucilla Sturges	23 Aug 1917
Glennie Daugherty	Lexie Smith	19 Aug 1917
W. M. Atchley	Mrs. Sarah Harrison	23 Aug 1917
Charley Smith	Mrs. Ida Williams	25 Aug 1917
Charles F. Harrison	Gracie Jackson	Date Not Shown
Arthur Read	Ina Akers	25 Jul 1917
Fred E. Chailland	Vallie Thompson	28 Aug 1917
Lee Higlin	Seler Gist	29 Aug 1917
W. H. Hoffman	Mary Margilee Whitworth	29 Aug 1917
W. N. Jones	Aline Connes	16 Aug 1917
Clason McGuire	Hester Williams	30 Aug 1917
O. H. Hodge	Mrs. Sallie Hart	30 Aug 1917
Carl Redburn	Katie Lomax	28 Aug 1917
Charley Patterson	Mabel Laster	2 Sep 1917
Tom Wheatley	Amy Minton	2 Sep 1917
Lee Nelson Gandoser	Verdie Webster	2 Sep 1917
J. R. Mize	**Mrs. Mary Green**	**6 Sep 1917**
Great great grandmother's third marriage		
Cecil Godwin	Myrtle Belver	2 Sep 1917
J. F. Morland	Susie Seeco	6 Sep 1917
William A. Miller	Ocel Gibson	9 Sep 1917
Leo Ford	Vera Bohanon	2 Sep 1917
Earnest Depe	Ettie Jones	9 Sep 1917
Jess Rogers	Don Eva Hearsum	8 Sep 1917
R. Arthur Laden	Gladys Copeland	9 Sep 1917
Paris E. Webb	Ethel McSparine	12 Sep 1917
Silas Newman	Emma Waddle	13 Sep 1917
J. R. (Bob) Parks	Lanora Basham	25 Aug 1917
Noah Bruce	Annie Alsman	15 Sep 1917
Alvie Herrell	Mrs. Hannah Herrell	15 Sep 1917
Willie S. Klien	Stella Higlin	13 Sep 1917
T. G. Stanfill	Mrs. Minnie Walker	16 Sep 1917
Johnie Miller	Mabel Dettrie	19 Sep 1917
Dilisle Godair	Amy R. Wicks	20 Sep 1917
W. T. McGue	Mrs. Catherine McCain	21 Sep 1917
Dee McConnaughey	Ada Stone	20 Sep 1917
Joseph G. Barnett	Nellie Frie	22 Sep 1917

GROOM	BRIDE	SOLEMNIZED
W. S. Roden	Dorothy Manly (Maney)	23 Sep 1917
J. W. Lomax	Prudence Riggs	20 Sep 1917
M. N. Howard	Mrs. Rosa Ashworth	1 Sep 1917
Clarence Ward	Katie Sanders	23 Sep 1917
Oscar W. Taylor	Leona Johnson	26 Sep 1917
O. C. Bradberry	Eula Atteberry	16 Sep 1917
D. C. Brooks	Lula Hasley	24 Sep 1917
Earnest Tompkins	Clara Palsgrove	25 Sep 1917
Oscar Krusey	Drucilla Perry	23 Sep 1917
William Hastings	Iva May Brydon	18 Sep 1917
James T. Dean	Mrs. Josephine Shipman	20 Sep 1917
C. A. Autrey	Mrs. Ethel B. Cross	26 Sep 1917
Martin J. Baird	Althea Mae Hall	26 Sep 1917
Clemens M. Lampe	Regina S. Peters	26 Sep 1917
Cleo Hilton	Della J. Nichols	21 Aug 1917
Charley D. Earle	Pearl Carter	30 Sep 1917
J. M. Grantham	Lilllian Bryant	27 Sep 1917
W. D. Gillespie	Mrs. Attie Storey	1 Oct 1917
William Rowland	Pearl Jones	22 Sep 1917
Alvis S. Holt	Elizabeth Hart	6 Oct 1917
Harry S. Sullivan	Lenna Lawrence	6 Oct 1917
Johnie Garner	Lucy Satterfield	12 Oct 1917
Albert Pierce	Beulah Jones	13 Oct 1917
W. D. Tankersley	Mrs. Mary Barton	17 Oct 1917
Wm. O'Brien	Mrs. Mary Yarbrough	19 Oct 1917
H. B. Parker	Alice Statler	12 Oct 1917
Will Connor	Stella Snider	21 Oct 1917
R. L. Gowan	Mrs. Nellie Sharp	22 Oct 1917
Thomas J. Stacy	Cora Davis	24 Sep 1917
W. H. Green (Greer)	Edith Bonnett	24 Oct 1917
Farris Denton	Mrs. Samila Lomax	19 Oct 1917
Louis Anderson	Dorie Herrman	16 Oct 1917
William Hardin Goodman	Mrs. Helen Christiana Hardin	20 Oct 1917
Charles F. Diggs	Alma Della Nation	13 Oct 1917
Charley L. Hendrixson	Ethel Eskew	3 Nov 1917
William L. Jones	Ethel Gibson	3 Nov 1917
John Osborn	Artie Stenneth	4 Nov 1917
Hessie R. Jenkins	Minnie Wilburn	4 Nov 1917
Edward Arnold	Lirlen Huggins	3 Nov 1917
Ed Anderson	Clara Jordan	7 Nov 1917
James W. Kizer	Hester Hill	2 Nov 1917
R. S. Wright	Allie Ridding	8 Nov 1917
Isom Waller	Minnie Martin	10 Nov 1917
B. E. B. Owens	Emma Lee Nation	11 Nov 1917

GROOM	BRIDE	SOLEMNIZED
F. B. Freeman	Gracie Hammonds	11 Nov 1917
Elmer L. Nation	Ester Page	6 Nov 1917
B. F. Hamrick	Clara Royer	10 Nov 1917
David Elmer Downs	Emma Attaberry	12 Nov 1917
Roy E. Canvey	Grace Cochrum	3 Oct 1917
Earl Kinser	Vernier Greer	14 Nov 1917
Elege Wheeler	Hattie McCracken	14 Nov 1917
A. N. Hays	Mrs. Flora Massey	10 Nov 1917
Charley Finley	Katie Pollard	18 Nov 1917
Duke Hargraves	Eva Elsworth	18 Nov 1917
Marshall Fisher	Biddie Johnson	18 Nov 1917
Clyde Holt	Ethel Hinnon	17 Nov 1917
William J. Butler	Pricy Lee	20 Nov 1917
S. F. Goodrich	Mrs. Mattie L. Jorden	24 Nov 1917
John Morgan	Mrs. Gertrude Vaughn	23 Nov 1917
B. F. Herren	Victoria Kelso	12 Nov 1917
Henry Smith	Mattie Richardson	5 Nov 1917
Chas. Curtis Barnes	Mrs. Iva M. Chandler	25 Nov 1917
W. R. Kimbrow	Elma Mable Turner	25 Nov 1917
Uther Britt	Annie Ballard	24 Nov 1917
Ora Bollinger	Bertha James	26 Nov 1917
S. J. Lairson	Mrs. Mary Johnson	26 Nov 1917
Benjamin A. Mathews	Mrs. Gertie Nunley	26 Nov 1917
Newton Ray	Nancy Hulens	25 Nov 1917
Earnest Lurber	Gertrude Curny	24 Nov 1917
Edgar Cude	Ruth Malone	29 Nov 1917
William Claud Caneer	Anna Laura Jones	9 Dec 1917
Carmack Wise	Willie Myers	21 Nov 1917
John Ruth	Allie Hembree	10 Dec 1917
L. O. Kirchen (Kinchen)	Hattie Buck	9 Dec 1917
Virgil Stewart	Flossie Renick	9 Dec 1917
Dallas Crud	Clarice Boon	14 Dec 1917
Charley Schram	Ora Back	14 Dec 1917
Owen Floyd Self	Glady Pearl Shrum	14 Dec 1917
Jack Wilson (col)	Girtie Moore (col)	16 Dec 1917
Jessie L. Hunter	Nellie V. Nadeny (Nading)	19 Dec 1917
Landon Rollins	Mrs. Georgia Jones	19 Dec 1917
Edd H. Casinger	Anna Tierce	20 Dec 1917
Joseph Steward	Manie Barber	11 Dec 1917
Emmitt T. Davis	J__ Petty	23 Dec 1917
Orville Engle	Ola Hutchenson	19 Dec 1917
C. Edgar Allen	Effie May Gargus	21 Dec 1917
William B. Swan	Francis Cooper	23 Dec 1917
Ralph Jones	Sallie G. Parnell	23 Nov 1917

GROOM	BRIDE	SOLEMNIZED
F. J. Vales	Marie Sanders	22 Dec 1917
Amon M. Ray	Alma B. Coons	25 Dec 1917
Tom Hays	Malissa Farrester (Forrester)	2 Dec 1917
Clyde M. Lane	Emma L. Gossage	26 Dec 1917
E. H. Lincoln	Ida Jackson	24 Dec 1917
J. E. Huggins	Ethel Taylor	25 Dec 1917
Andrew Gurley	Myrtle Davidson	27 Dec 1917
J. N. Campbell	Mrs. Belle Weakley	27 Dec 1917
Thomas Murphy	Hattie Parsons	24 Dec 1917
Marvin E. Thornsberry	Ida Lee Wyatt	27 Dec 1917
Frank Shelton Darylor	Hallie Woods	30 Dec 1917
James B. Meharg	Effie Williamson	26 Dec 1917
Otto Freeman	Bertha Neeley	30 Dec 1917
Luther Elder	Sallie Beard	8 Dec 1917
W. F. Brannum Jr.	Mrs. Annie Parker	29 Dec 1917
B. H. Southard	Ida Davis	30 Dec 1917
Edgar Wood	Maudie Kelley	30 Dec 1917
Clarence Beavers	Mrs. Maude Beauchamp	16 Feb 1918
J. A. Hardy	Rosy Day	14 Feb 1918
Everett B. Mobley	Josie Aileene Donaldson	13 Jan 1918
Geo. F. King	Effie Scott	23 Dec 1917
Wilburn Templeton	Grace Green	6 Jan 1918
Samuel S. Schaffer	Elna Parsons	30 Dec 1917
Robert C. Carter	Minnie Griffin	28 Dec 1917
Z. T. Kelley	Mrs. Valley Smith	23 Dec 1917
James W. Tripp	Velva M. Rees	15 Jan 1918
Chas. A. Wells	Nannye Osborne	12 Jan 1918
C. H. Baker	Eva Mills	17 Jan 1918
W. D. Spencer	Mrs. Sarah Gooch	17 Jan 1918
W. M. Mason	Chloe M. Pottilla	2 Dec 1917
Ed Wheeler	Carrie Mikel	19 Jan 1918
Alexander Ellis	Mrs. Addie Anderson	22 Jan 1918
Kid Emerson	Mrs. Martha C. Davis	12 Jan 1918
C. A. Sale	Ocie Duckett	23 Jan 1918
Chas. A. Fulton	Mrs. Abbie Fulton	28 Jan 1918
Oscar C. Fuzzell	Bertha Johnson	27 Jan 1918
John Fitzgerald	Belle Morgan	26 Jan 1918
Robert L. Craig	Vallie Williams	28 Jan 1918
Otis McNeil	Mrs. Josie Honeycutt	29 Jan 1918
Ralph E. Walker	Margaret B. Campbell	30 Nov 1917
Thomas Bass	Gertie Myers	31 Jan 1918
Riley McDaniel	May Bell Crawley	13 Jan 1918
Steve Hicks	Belle Herrington	25 Jan 1918
Homer Kennedy	Mrs. Maddie Barham	23 Jan 1918

GROOM	BRIDE	SOLEMNIZED
Gus. H. Ridings	Edith C. Masters	3 Feb 1918
Willie Lewis	Pearl Peerman	10 Jan 1918
Elmer C. Bridges	Lillie Howard	2 Feb 1918
Cleveland C. McKinzie	Mamie L. Belt	3 Feb 1918
C. H. Dunning	Lillie Blackenter	7 Feb 1918
E. S. Foster	Lottie Harp	30 Nov 1917
Lenley N. Hall	Pearl Church	4 Feb 1918
T. H. Queen	Mrs. Mary L. Rodgers	6 Feb 1918
Bruce O'dell	Estella Barber	22 Dec 1917
Holly Lee Gore	Mrs. Mary Jane Taylor	7 Feb 1918
C. E. McDale	Dollie Lancaster	7 Feb 1918
Dave Shelton	Fannie Beavers	7 Feb 1918
Henry Cambron	Mrs. Zura Marcum	11 Feb 1918
Lee A. Lemonds	Edith O. Bilderback	10 Feb 1918
H. J. Haas	Mrs. Etta Vail	10 Feb 1918
C. A. Everton	Sallie Lamb	12 Feb 1918
Thomas Hall	Mrs. Allie M. Neal	14 Feb 1918
P. Frank Smith	Edith White	13 Feb 1918
Andy Craft	Rebecca Lale	18 Feb 1918
J. M. Milstead	Mrs. Julia Cunningham	18 Feb 1918
S. B. Richardson	Vessie L. Wilburn	23 Dec 1917
Noble Seabaugh	Laura Ezell	17 Feb 1918
Marcus C. Wilkins	Beryl Goodwin	18 Feb 1918
Grover S. Price	Luna Petty	18 Feb 1918
P. L. Parker	Ethel Stacy	21 Feb 1918
Powell M. Snow	Renah Edwards	20 Feb 1918
J. E. Vaughn	Alice Waganer	21 Feb 1918
R. R. Raines	Beulah Perry	20 Feb 1918
Earl Thomas	Lola Mango	23 Feb 1918
John A. Hall	Alice Ramsey	24 Feb 1918
Darwin Irwin	Cecil Walker	23 Feb 1918
Clarence Jenkins	Flora Mangale	27 Feb 1918
S. J. Malone	Martha Whitlock	27 Feb 1918
Robert C. Clark	Bertha L. White	2 Mar 1918
W. A. Reagan	Mrs. Mamie Churchwell	6 Mar 1918
W. M. Ladyman	Delia Pugh	6 Mar 1918
Henry Meadows	Lottie Boyer	6 Mar 1918
Ester Smith	Zettie Hale	7 Mar 1918
Richard Morrison	Pansey Ferguson	11 Mar 1918
Charley Hill	Francis Smith	10 Mar 1918
John Whitlock	Maggie Gibson	13 Mar 1918
L. V. Davis	Mrs. Rachel Wagoner	2 Mar 1918
Earnest L. Perry	Mrs. Sadie Scott	27 Feb 1918
Robert Brinkley	Violet Ellis	2 Mar 1918

GROOM	BRIDE	SOLEMNIZED
John Balgenorth	Eva Lemonds	9 Mar 1918
F. M. Hughes	Mrs. Ivy Jennings	12 Mar 1918
Geo. R. Thomas	Rosy Mangold	16 Mar 1918
T. F. Taylor	Mrs. Eva Simpson	20 Feb 1918
Arthur Pinkston	Dollie Donica	13 Mar 1918
Harry Lewis	Nellie Aldrich	6 Mar 1918
Thomas L. Powell	Ollie A. Dowdy	23 Mar 1918
Cris Hart	Pena Vincent	23 Mar 1918
E. P. Benson	Mrs. Nola Sexton	21 Mar 1918
F. C. Strong	Gertie Thompson	20 Mar 1918
Purl C. Wright	Gladys Johnson	23 Mar 1918
Loye Gawner	Merideth Reynolds	20 Feb 1918
Lim Cope	Mrs. Nettie Pearl Hampton	25 Mar 1918
Sam Griffin	Mrs. Mable Williams	26 Mar 1918
J. E. Piercy	Mrs. Emma Wright	24 Mar 1918
Rolla Perry	Vietta Lewis	30 Mar 1918
John Rushin	Viena Ray	31 Mar 1918
Chester C. Washington	Mary Temperence Bradley	31 Mar 1918
M. A. Hyde	Stella Howard	5 Apr 1918
John McIllwain	Mrs. Florence Hill	2 Apr 1918
Marion French	Lottie Wadely	30 Mar 1918
Marion Schaffar	Mrs. Lillie Thomann	23 Mar 1918
J. W. Liddell	Myrtle Roberts	27 Mar 1918
W. S. Hill	Nettie Berry	27 Mar 1918
Beauford Green	Lydie Turnham (Turnbon)	31 Mar 1918
William Byers	Mrs. Nancy C. Kramer	19 Mar 1918
Bee Boone	Beulah Preslar	30 Mar 1918
J. W. Blankenship	Mrs. Rena Kirby	20 Apr 1918
Roy Blocker	Beedie Carter	20 Apr 1918
W. C. Clark	Vera Lockard	14 Apr 1918
Jessie Fleetwood	Lew Crowell	10 Apr 1918
Loy Hurn	Myrtle Smith	13 Apr 1918
J. F. Hendrix	Myrtle Ellis	21 Apr 1918
Frank Heurell (Henrell)	Bessie Gibson	4 May 1918
Andrew Jordan	Ethel Hatcher	19 Apr 1918
Edgar Killion	Ora Mangold	5 May 1918
Geo. McDaniel	Ora Groves	15 Apr 1918
L. O. Pierce	India May Ellis	1 May 1918
Jim Renfro	Effie Madison	21 Apr 1918
Dell R. Stephens	Ova Powell	2 May 1918
G. L. Young	Mrs. Laura Oldham	10 Apr 1918
Rola Taylor	Leona Ayers	11 Apr 1918
C. E. Vaughn	Mrs. Maggie Gregory	18 Apr 1918
James Willis	Ella Mitchell	16 Apr 1918

GROOM	BRIDE	SOLEMNIZED
A. P. Wilson	Mrs. Crisey Verble	2 May 1918
Fred Trease	Thelma Cravatt	30 Apr 1918
W. H. Wright	Sylvia L. Hoxworth	5 May 1918
Clarence W. Clark	Holdie May Summers	8 May 1918
Paul McClain	Wheeler Sandefur	5 May 1918
Joe Kitrel	Ollie Ray Edwards	7 May 1918
James P. King	Sarah Ann Masters	12 May 1918
Horace Basil Boyd	Carrie Lucile Wheeler	11 May 1918
Justice H. Carmack	Lona L. Hart	25 May 1918
Dann E. Derr	Dallie Calls	25 May 1918
Boyd Dowdy	Ethel McNabb	24 May 1918
Van Edwards	Agnes Trecie Malinda Perryman	25 May 1918
John Herrell	Stella Haldbreak	28 May 1918
Seabert Myers	Mrs. Elsie Raden	3 Jun 1918
Levi A. Neal	Nola Romines	2 Jun 1918
Clarence Price	Leona Williams	1 Jun 1918
Walter Snider	Rosie Folks	8 Jun 1918
William E. Jones	Bessie Gibson	8 Jun 1918
Fred D. Mason	Lucy Bell Johnson	9 Jun 1918
Hilery Evans	Bertha Laden	7 Jun 1918
Curtis Moore	Hattie Cuningham	20 Jun 1918
W. F. Kelney(Kelvey)	Mrs. Velma Buthcer	20 Jun 1918
John Wesley Owens	Mrs. Lizzie Dudley	11 Apr 1918
C. W. Brewsaugh	Mrs. Maggie Onan	18 Jun 1918
Jim Stone	Mary Louise Van Trease	8 Jun 1918
Davied Paul	Mrs. Edna Riley	15 Jun 1918
William A. Pearson	Roxie Bennett	15 Jun 1918
John Bruireley	Lela Whitehead	17 Jun 1918
Joe P. Whitlock	Maude M. Oats	19 Jun 1918
Jim M. Ezell	Mrs. Macy Alice Hall	22 Jun 1918
Joe Yates	Jessie Lynn Wade	26 Jun 1918
Jessie Reeves	Mrs. Artie Martin	2 Jul 1918
James T. Robinett	Mary L. Kendrick	10 Apr 1918
Ora Moore	Georgia Lee Whitten	4 Jul 1918
F. M. Yow	Mrs. Lena Webster	10 Jul 1918
W. T. Redman	Mrs. Ella S. Daily	5 Jul 1918
Jeff Sinclair	Sallie Melton	10 Jul 1918
Charlie Trice	Mrs. S. V. Ayers	15 Jul 1918
G. A. Fife	Laura Carr	16 Jul 1918
J. E. Rush	Deliah E. Meyers	18 Jul 1918
Tom Jarrett	Ethel Woods	18 Jul 1918
Elvie E. Snider	Minnie M. Appell	20 Jul 1918
Benj. F. Matthews	Mrs. Gertie Nunley	20 Jul 1918
Edward V. McGraw Jr.	Hattie M. Jorden	13 Jul 1918

GROOM	BRIDE	SOLEMNIZED
O. R. Drake	Bertha Curry	4 Jul 1918
R. T. Braden	Katie Groomes	15 Jul 1918
Harvey L. Smith	Mary Casey	23 Jul 1918
Delbert C. Akers	Stella M. Cable	27 Jul 1918
W. T. Kerr	Mrs. Mary Clark	27 Jul 1918
Sam Jackson	Bessie Goodman	28 Jul 1918
J. L. Hampton	Mrs. Louanna Stephens	23 Jul 1918
Sam J. Cook	Mrs. Lucy Powers	19 Jul 1918
Lee Shelton	Mrs. Kelly Vinson	18 Jul 1918
W. P. Conts (Coats, Couts)	Mrs. Belle Rogers	Date Not Shown
Myrton E. Ormsbee	Verda V. Knight	21 Jul 1918
Melvin Proffer	Ethel Hicks	26 Jul 1918
Henry Ed Pierce	Mrs. Onba Walker	30 Jul 1918
Thos. E. Cooper	Bonnie Charlton	1 Aug 1918
Chester _. Bilderback	Mary Walker	4 Aug 1918
L. A. McLesky	Myrtle Holthouser	27 Jul 1918
Jessie Sanford	Ethel Neal	4 Aug 1918
Ezra A. Mangold	Della Riess	31 Aug 1918
W. W. Kinny	Mrs. Lula Williams	6 Aug 1918
Lexie Bryan Hampton	Mabel Kathleen Lucas	27 Jul 1918
J. W. Denbow	Mrs. L. L. Caudel	6 Aug 1918
Harley Dean	Ida Williams	6 Aug 1918
O. A. Bratcher	Nellie Neighbors	7 Aug 1918
Jessie Black (Block)	Maude L. Mayer	7 Aug 1918
Edgar O. Rowtov	Dallie Bradshaw	10 Aug 1918
Euther O. Bird	Gertrude O'Connor	9 Jun 1918
Geo. Dewey Faultner	Vivian Cooper	15 Jun 1918
C. J. Key	Iva Grissom	8 Aug 1918
Almreen Hays	Mamie L. Petty	4 Aug 1918
Sam Holloway	Hellen Crider	10 Aug 1918
A. G. Shrum	**Mrs. Alice Hendricks**	**11 Aug 1918**
(great grandfather on father's mother's side)		
Leon Stone	Bertha Lackey	12 Aug 1918
G. M. Johnson	Fannie Goldsmith	12 Aug 1918
Roscoe Paul	Mary Stout	14 Aug 1918
Harry Elliott	Minnie Ball	12 Jul 1918
Elmer Myers	Mrs. Martha Coplin	17 Jul 1918
J. C. Trosper	Ida Dement	14 Aug 1918
W. T. Carter	Lillie Wilbanks	17 Aug 1918
Alva Abbott	Bertha Bone (Bane)	17 Aug 1918
E. R. Hendrix	Mrs. Lucy McGuire	21 Aug 1918
Frank Pierce	Lillie D. Pitman	7 Aug 1918
W. N. Marr	Mrs. Ollie Lynn	24 Aug 1918
Edward L. Harrison	Bessie M. Hogland	15 May 1918

GROOM	BRIDE	SOLEMNIZED
Elmer Lane	Omer Gentry	8 May 1918
John Moore	Mrs. Dara Vennett	24 Aug 1918
J. W. Singleton	Mrs. May White	31 Aug 1918
Robert F. Parr	Lela Shaw	2 Sep 1918
William Lawnsdale	Ottilee Philpot	1 Sep 1918
Rolley E. Derr	Janie C. Cubbage	4 Aug 1918
G. C. Wadley	Rena Blocker	24 Aug 1918
Elmer Eubanks	Edith Malone	30 Aug 1918
Isaac N. Pharr	Mrs. Rhode Kennedy	11 Sep 1918
S. A. Marshall	Etta M. Baker	12 Sep 1918
W. M. Harrell	Vernia Casey	1 Sep 1918
B. F. Norman	Willa J. Young	14 Sep 1918
James D. Maglove	Agnes Felty	16 Sep 1918
W. F. Gerhardt	Mrs. Ione Rosenwater	14 Sep 1918
R. D. Aurbed	Della Vanover	19 Sep 1918
Bert B. Qurman	Mrs. Osie Fletcher	16 Sep 1918
J. A. Allison	Pearl Clay	21 Sep 1918
I. D. Williams	Mrs. Myrtle House	21 Sep 1918
John N. Crutchfield	Connie Cash	26 Sep 1918
C. J. Southern	Mrs. Minnie Cowens	18 Sep 1918
Clyde H. Micare	Myrtle M. Shepard	27 Sep 1918
Alfred L. Emory	Mary Gordon	27 Sep 1918
John Atnip	Jennie Bills	28 Sep 1918
Hugh Berry	Nola Louie	2 Oct 1918
W. F. Acree	Alma Lawson	3 Oct 1918
James S. Deason	Mrs. Nora L. Fikuart	12 Oct 1918
Brodie Redden	Annie Long	16 Aug 1918
Rosevelt Shaw (col)	Emma Durham(col)	13 Oct 1918
John H. Raney	Gertrude E. Smith	13 Oct 1918
Leroy Davis	Mayme Morrow	15 Oct 1918
D. B. Brown	Mrs. Annie Estes	24 Aug 1918
W. R. Jenkins	Mrs. Rosie Bradshaw	28 Aug 1918
Everett Jackson	Mrs. Addie Stewart	3 Oct 1918
Ollie Lee Long	Cora M. Walker	16 Oct 1918
Lawton Nuckles	Eura Garner	2 Sep 1918
Claude Pelts	Mary Ethel Kirby	13 Oct 1918
Robert Fish	Mrs. Gracie Harrison	19 Oct 1918
Gid. D. Fish	Mrs. Neldie Disher	23 Oct 1918
James K. P. Whitrow	Mrs. Melvina Ray	8 Oct 1918
Roscoe Hampton	Belle Pollard	19 Oct 1918
Arnold Elsworth	Oddie Hargraves	27 Oct 1918
John M. Lancaster	Agnes E. Scobey	26 Oct 1918
Everett Wilkerson	Florrie Pigman	4 Nov 1918
Chas. Elton Hartle	Dora Beatrice Pigman	4 Nov 1918

GROOM	BRIDE	SOLEMNIZED
James Harrison Smith	Alta Sanders	7 Nov 1918
M. S. Revelle	Nora Stanfield	5 Nov 1918
Willie v. Lanier	Gertrude Palmer	7 Nov 1918
Edward S. Stark	Evelyn Yarbrough	12 Oct 1918
Chas. Cato	Celia E. Watson	12 Nov 1918
A. F. Pierce	Annie Cook	14 Nov 1918
H. Beshears	Mrs. Jolie Bennett	17 Nov 1918
Arthur P. Parker	Della May Samples	20 Nov 1918
Wm. H. Burkett	Maggie Tilson	23 Nov 1918
James E. Goodin	Nettie May Sovarmes	23 Nov 1918
Clarence Easley	Elsie May Cowens	23 Nov 1918
Wheeler A. Culbertson	Geertrude Myers	23 Nov 1918
John M. Wilburn	Lena Belle Cagle	23 Nov 1918
Zack Davis	Nettie Jackson	23 Nov 1918
Edgar Stratman	Mary Stenger	26 Nov 1918
L. C. Pagan	Madge Somers	28 Nov 1918
S. T. McGlawn	Golda Baughn	30 Nov 1918
G. W. Gallion	Annie Aidelott	8 Nov 1918
Horace Edwards	Mary J. Onan	1 Dec 1918
Audie W. Wagner	Clara Bennett	30 Nov 1918
Clarence Peeler	Maggie Dudley	1 Dec 1918
John H. Hughs	June E. Bridges	30 Nov 1918
J. H. Killion	Gracie Lee Emer__	3 Dec 1918
Marshall Arthur	Gillie Ann Gooch	1 Dec 1918
Harry Fleener	Myrtle Guthrey	3 Dec 1918
J. H. Anderson	Mrs. Julia Jones	17 Nov 1918
John L. Miller	Maude Bailey	7 Dec 1918
William L. Blackburn	Mary Emory Eaton	30 Nov 1918
Edward McQuaid	Mrs. Alice V. Slant	10 Dec 1918
Dewey Miles	Nettie Ray	8 Dec 1918
Christopher Masters	Mrs Janie White	8 Dec 1918
W. W. Houston	Gillie Bodine	7 Dec 1918
Albert Lane	Myrtle Lee Wilkerson	13 Dec 1918
O. B. Burnett	Effie Baker	15 Dec 1918
Charley Tidwell	Mrs. Nola Collins	15 Dec 1918
Bob Morrison	Clatha Strout	14 Dec 1918
Delbert Messmore	Annie Tally	8 Dec 1918
Leonard Low	Ona May McNew	15 Dec 1918
Alvis Fleetwood	Annie Bell Petty	15 Dec 1918
Thos. A. Dallin	Rosa P. Hankins	13 Dec 1918
S. A. Lovelace	Myrtle Hurst	7 Dec 1918
Wade Manley	Strandie Harris	9 Dec 1918
Fred E. Doherty	Bulah Reeves	23 Nov 1918
W. P. Earls	Edith C. Eakers	17 Dec 1918

GROOM	BRIDE	SOLEMNIZED
Roy Harman	Agness Herren	19 Dec 1918
Earl McDaniel	Iler Easley	8 Oct 1918
Guy M. Bennett	Minnie Baugher	21 Dec 1918
Ben F. Lewis	Tempie L. Pruit	14 Dec 1918
Martin Snider	Lona Vincent	22 Dec 1918
Lewis Mosley	Mattiie M. Killian	25 Dec 1918
Leslie Hardin	Edna Kelley	25 Dec 1918
W. F. Horner	Lue D. Casinger	25 Dec 1918
David M. Ragsdale	Anna Lucas	25 Dec 1918
C. H. Mitchell	Florence Cashon	25 Dec 1918
Jas. M. Harris	Mrs. Belle Clemens	14 Dec 1918
Ben F. Smith	Nell Kitchell	14 Dec 1918
Philip P. Bowen	Myrtle C. Wallace	22 Dec 1918
Agno Dutty	Mrs. Ada Vaughn	26 Dec 1918
Gustavus Lasswell	G. Meriam Ely	28 Dec 1918
Grattie Ramsey	Myrtle M. Billips	23 Dec 1918
C. H. Acord	Stella Highlander	23 Dec 1918
Chas. H. Estridge	Ethel Wallace	30 Dec 1918
Archie L. Porterfield	Bethel Ballard	28 Dec 1918
W. T. Emery	Emer Weeks	6 Jan 1919
Chas. E. Haddon	Myrtle McNeil	6 Jan 1919
S. A. Oliver	Ethel Ponder	5 Jan 1919
J. R. Killion	Parlee Hahn	2 Jan 1919
S. S. Frederick	Mary J. Lemasters	1 Jan 1919
I. G. Scarbrough	Ella Causey	2 Jan 1919
_. M. Dalton	Mrs. Jennie Smith	8 Jan 1919
George W. Henson	Laura Hughes	5 Jan 1919
Charley Thompson	Mary Cadle	11 Jan 1919
Melvin Pugh	Mattie Gwaltney	14 Jan 1919
T. M. Robbins	Mrs. Clara Randels	12 Jan 1919
Louis Nichols	Esther Toole	11 Jan 1919
James Whitworth	Myrtle Lynn	14 Jan 1919
William Johnson	Kate Jameson	11 Jan 1919
John Ray	Lue Biggs	9 Jan 1919
Mitchell Johnson	Essie Fallwell	11 Jan 1919
Emanuel Hodge	Lena Ward	14 Jan 1919
John M. Williams	Mrs. S. D. Lamb	12 Jan 1919
J. W. Paxton	Mrs. May Hagges	23 Dec 1918
Will Esters	Ethel Kirkwood	27 Dec 1918
Alonzo Rye	Mollie Regor	7 Jan 1919
William H. Hollifield	Vivian Ruth Cook	5 Oct 1918
E. Martin	Claudie Rodgers	24 Jan 1919
Joe H. Thompson	Bouton Wells	23 Dec 1918
Burley F. Crawford	Mary Etta Muse	1 Feb 1919

GROOM	BRIDE	SOLEMNIZED
William Adams	Truete Horn	2 Feb 1919
Tim Waddell	Mrs. Elvis Detry	26 Jan 1919
S. C. Rose	Gladys Ross	9 Feb 1919
T. L. Roark	Julia Campbell	8 Feb 1919
Marcus Williams	Mandie Myricks	9 Feb 1919
William R. Plunkett	Elizabeth Walker	24 Dec 1918
T. H. Bridges	Mrs. Lee Ire	8 Feb 1919
Herman Eubanks	Tena Rash	5 Feb 1919
John Garrison	Buck Ezell	28 Jan 1919
Daniel Lawson	Ruth Davis	10 Feb 1919
J. R. Huggins	Rose Williford	10 Feb 1919
Ossey Maples	Della Kinsey	23 Jan 1919
W. A. Conder	Hattie Utley	26 Jan 1919
Claude H. Luckett	Lora Waltrip	25 Jan 1919
Jim Enox	Iva Hicks	27 Jan 1919
Lenard Rodeck	Mrs. Mary Mopkin	28 Jan 1919
F. J. Moore	Tennie Davis	7 Feb 1919
Mathew Gunter	Ruth Eubanks	13 Feb 1919
Clarence Tate	Bessie Duke	18 Jan 1919
John L. Smith	Martha Gulledge	18 Jan 1919
Ray Lowery	Anne Hurt	19 Jan 1919
Clifford Dover	Anne Hurt	18 Jan 1919
Nathan Conyers	Pearl Holmes	19 Jan 1919
Laurence Stroble	Ella Miner	12 Feb 1919
Theodore Hollaway	Anna Gargus	9 Feb 1919
John Danson	Sendy Kirby	9 Feb 1919
John Lairson	Clara Kagius	20 Jan 1919
Robert H. Stone	Myrtle Rawsey	13 Feb 1919
Ray Coats	Anna Worthing	11 Feb 1919
James T. Sisk	Bertha May Copeland	12 Feb 1919
Samy S. O'daniel	Bessie Smith	13 Feb 1919
William R. Bazar	Mary Rutley	12 Feb 1919
Claude Thomas	Lowell Robinson	15 Feb 1919
Chas. King	Effie Parrent	16 Feb 1919
Henry Kroes	Lelia Birmingham	18 Feb 1919
Elbert Butler	Ruth Moore	8 Mar 1919
G. M. Baxter	Mrs. Minnie L. Fields	1 Mar 1919
Edmond Baker	Leona Pruit	20 Feb 1919
Allen Collins	Bessie Berryman	23 Feb 1919
Herman Cato	Ida Goodman	15 Mar 1919
J. _. Dye	Virgie Hart	20 Mar 1919
Walter Frost	Rachel Nicholas	16 Mar 1919
John W. Harvey	Minnie M. Cullins	20 Feb 1919
Bluford H. Hendrix	Rosie Knight	25 Feb 1919

GROOM	BRIDE	SOLEMNIZED
Billie Hampton	Pearl St. Clair	4 Mar 1919
Robert Henson	Frankie Barnes	23 Feb 1919
Louis Harman	Caroline Myers	3 Mar 1919
W. W. Irie	Ella Shafe	1 Mar 1919
Lew Jones	Bernice Poe	2 Mar 1919
Luther J. Johnson	Gladys Singleton	16 Mar 1919
Forest Jones	Ruth Dublin	2 Mar 1919
W. H. Mizell	Eva Burns	16 Mar 1919
Charley McWorthey	Annie Berkley	25 Feb 1919
Hershel E. Pool	Nettie Williams	13 Mar 1919
William Redman	Hattie Mungle	7 Mar 1919
J. C. Stars	Esther M. Jackson	17 Feb 1919
Herman F. Stewart	Florence E. Livers	26 Feb 1919
Harry Smith	Dora Herrell	18 Mar 1919
R. W. Vowel	Essie Long	20 Feb 1919
Claude Williams	Dona Austion	1 Mar 1919
William A. Walker	Pearl Henson	9 Mar 1919
D. H. Whitlock	Mrs. Mannie Hodge	23 Mar 1919
Floyd Stonum	Eva Wood	21 Mar 1919
Kirby Dockins	Leatha Hamilton	21 Mar 1919
Laurence Harris	Ethel Dodson	17 Mar 1919
John Bledsoe	Elizabeth Gordon	1 Mar 1919
Walter Carter	Grace Hicks	18 Mar 1919
George Mitchell	Mrs. Mary Trantham	7 Apr 1919
T. J. Davis	Donna Shelton	2 Apr 1919
John Lincoln	Mrs. Minnie Page	17 Jan 1919
Walter Wilburn	Edna Bucbanav	23 Mar 1919
E. A. Terry	Sarah B. McGuire	3 Apr 1919
I. H. Hayes	Emmie Pool	1 Apr 1919
Coy George	Ula Jackson	21 Mar 1919
Will Boss	Edna Jaye	29 Mar 1919
Monroe Godby	Mrs. Maggie Cobb	28 Mar 1919
Roy C. Cook	Verne Napper	28 Mar 1919
Roy Scott	Loviece Talley	29 Mar 1919
Fred Allen	Zella Barks	31 Mar 1919
James Farmer	Susie Wadkins	22 Mar 1919
C. J. Ruddee	Lizzie E. Richardson	7 Apr 1919
Cleve Lacey	Beulah Reid (Reed)	9 Apr 1919
Paul Teetrs	Mrs. Rebecca James	5 Apr 1919
Arthur Brannon	Martie Bell Veach	6 Apr 1919
Chas. Mugent (Nugent)	Luella Bunton	9 Apr 1919
Tom Garrett	Stive Lemonds	10 Apr 1919
Oristo Paschall	Ruth Parsons	8 Apr 1919
Henry Arusman	Mrs. Jennie Webb	5 Apr 1919

GROOM	BRIDE	SOLEMNIZED
Lee Riley	Mrs. Cula Smith	14 Apr 1919
Harry E. Avery	Ada May Avery	14 Apr 1919
W. F. Benson	A. C. Hicks	13 Apr 1919
Albert Sandefur	Maud Cook	15 Apr 1919
John C. Brown	Lovie Shrum	16 Apr 1919
William Stakes	Edith Pearson	19 Apr 1919
J. F. Stubblefield	Mrs. Rosa Boyd	22 Apr 1919
Oscar Haire	Grace Welty	17 Apr 1919
J. McCloud	Lena Finch	24 Apr 1919
George Holder	Ada Crosno	18 Apr 1919
G. W. Palmer	Fannie Edwards	19 Apr 1919
Lloyd Butler	Bessie Wallace	25 Apr 1919
Jim Hughes	Jennie Beckham	25 Apr 1919
Cornelius Scott	Mrs. Anna Bruce	22 Apr 1919
Samuel R. Frederick	Georgia Lee Young	26 Apr 1919
Tarrance A. Jaynes	Mellie Tolbert	26 Apr 1919
Jonathan French	Jessie Sisk	26 Apr 1919
H. C. Hampton	Easter Short	28 Apr 1919
James Stallions	Mrs. Ada Voss	27 Apr 1919
Henry A. Acree	Velma Sisson	4 May 1919
W. C. Cagle	Nancy Mayo Stanfield	1 May 1919
Luther E. Coley	Lottie Coley	5 May 1919
John H. Gately	Lottie May Miller	5 May 1919
G. W. Moore	Clara McDaniel	7 May 1919
Chalen A. Nelson	Emmer Crawley	6 May 1919
Philip M. Sherman	Mary Edith Peeler	4 May 1919
A. H. Smith	Effie Green	6 May 1919
Hubert A. Wise	Mrs. Elizabeth Wiland	28 Apr 1919
Earnest F. Wells	Billie Davis	30 Apr 1919
S. U. Wilson	Beatrice Fraizer	4 May 1919
James E. Davis	Lucell Lowery	26 May 1919
John W. Hall	Dollie Goodman	19 May 1919
Virgil A. O'Connor	Blanche Pollard	21 May 1919
Mike Price	Nellie Hutchinson	21 May 1919
Aytch Bowman	Beatrice Sneed	18 May 1919
Ray Rogers	Pearl Smedley	11 May 1919
Elmer Smith	Mrs. Myrtle Parten	24 May 1919
W. C. Keller	Georgia Wyricks	24 May 1919
Arthur Moore	Ellen French	14 May 1919
Bennie Alson Pavey	Lillie May Price	12 May 1919
John Conn	Pansey Waters	13 May 1919
John Vance	Gertie Moore	9 May 1919
Orley Stroud	Ethel M. Davis	17 May 1919
Joseph G. Hustedde	Margareth H. Eberhardt	7 May 1919

GROOM	BRIDE	SOLEMNIZED
John Huskey	Mrs. Dela Walker	12 May 1919
Hersel Romines	Clyde Brewer	10 May 1919
C. E. Blair	Mrs. Bertha Ray	26 May 1919
James R. Cato	Ruth E. Knight	1 Jun 1919
Robert Capps	Nerlice Merritt	7 Jun 1919
Arthur Cox	Earley Wagster	10 May 1919
N. A. Douglass	Iva Byrell	16 May 1919
Charley Greenfield	Viola Eakins	2 Jun 1919
Carl C. Howard	Irene Steel	27 May 1919
John Herron	Mrs. Norneer Davenport	8 Jun 1919
J. O. Bryant (O'Bryant)	Beatrice Collins	1 Jun 1919
Carl Pedego	Iva Mince	1 Jun 1919
William Richardson	May Bell Cagle	8 May 1919
Oliver Shrum	Lola L. Pitts	7 Jun 1919
Hugh Ray	Jennie Smith	8 Jun 1919
Arthur Acree	Martha Deniston	15 Jun 1919
Geo. Boss	Callie Washburn	15 Jun 1919
W. C. Coburn	Lee Mayberry	22 Jun 1919
Willie Davis	Darcia Dellingham	21 Jun 1919
Albert Gardner	Mrs. Mary Tanner	21 Jun 1919
George Hampton	Esther Buck	12 Jun 1919
Orville Haywood	Ethel Emery	18 Jun 1919
B. F. Hammond	Luler Bowden	14 Jun 1919
Fred Hall	Nell Blanche Adams	15 Jun 1919
H. H. Hardison	Angie May Davis	27 May 1919
Otto L. Miner	Joeanni_e Miller	10 Jun 1919
Oscar Moore	Myrtle Meek	22 Jun 1919
Grover McCage	Mrs. Bertha Kilbreath	26 May 1919
William E. Noaks	Lela Baxter	12 Jun 1919
G. Truman Rice	Genia Rose Scarff	1 Jun 1919
Harry Skaggs	Mrs. Fannie Askew	14 Jun 1919
George Yount	Ada White	14 Jun 1919
John Beaver	Mrs. Bertha Pierce	21 Jun 1919
Harry Beckel	Vivian Greer	5 Jul 1919
James A. Clark	Mrs. Kate Dosier	24 Jun 1919
W. D. Collins	Mrs. Maude Bowman	28 Jun 1919
Harvey Cunningham	Dora Prossell	6 Jul 1919
William B. Crash	Mrs. Hattie Muse	10 Jun 1919
H. A. Depew	Mrs. Cora Depew	22 Jun 1919
Thomas Edwards	Gladys Carpenter	24 Jun 1919
William T. Green	Hellen Shelton	8 Jul 1919
Fred Hendrix	Emely Willis	27 Jun 1919

Abbott, 15
Acord, 1, 6, 18
Acree, 16, 21-22
Acuff, 3
Adams, 19, 22
Adkins, 6
Aidelott, 17
Akers, 8, 15
Akins, 6
Alberson, 7
Aldrich, 13
Allen, 2-3, 6-7, 10, 20
Allison, 16
Alsman, 8
Alsup, 5
Anders, 4
Anderson, 9, 11, 17
Anthony, 2
Appell, 14
Arnold, 1, 3, 6-9
Arr, 7
Arthur, 17
Arusman, 20
Ashworth, 1, 9
Askew, 22
Atchley, 8
Athelton, 7
Atnip, 16
Attaberry, 10
Atteberry, 9
Aurbed, 16
Austin, 1
Austion, 20
Autrey, 5, 9
Avery, 21
Ayers, 13-14
Back, 10
Bailey, 5-7, 17
Baird, 9
Baker, 3-4, 6-7, 11, 16-17

Baker, 3
Balgenorth, 13
Ball, 15
Ballard, 10, 18
Bane, 5, 15
Barah, 4
Barbee, 3
Barber, 10, 12
Barham, 4, 11
Barks, 20
Barnes, 10, 20
Barnett, 8
Barron, 6
Barton, 9
Basham, 8
Bass, 11
Bassett, 2
Batchelor, 3
Baugher, 1, 18
Baughn, 17
Baxter, 19, 22
Bazar, 19
Beard, 11
Beauchamp, 11
Beaver, 22
Beavers, 11-12
Beckel, 22
Beckham, 21
Beggs, 4
Behr, 7
Bell, 4, 7
Belle, 4
Belt, 12
Belver, 8
Bennett, 14, 17-18
Benson, 1, 13, 21
Berkley, 20
Berry, 13, 16
Berryman, 19
Beshears, 17
Biggs, 18

Bighan, 1
Bilderback, 12, 15
Billips, 18
Bills, 16
Bird, 15
Birmingham, 19
Bishop, 4
Bitticks, 1
Black, 15
Blackburn, 17
Blackenter, 12
Blair, 22
Blakemore, 1-2
Blankenship, 13
Bledsoe, 20
Block, 15
Blocker, 13, 16
Bodine, 17
Bohannon, 8
Bollinger, 10
Bone, 15
Bonnett, 9
Boon, 10
Boone, 13
Boozer, 3
Borah, 7
Boss, 20, 22
Bostwick, 7
Bowden, 3, 22
Bowen, 18
Bowman, 21-22
Boyd, 1, 14, 21
Boyer, 12
Bradberry, 9
Braden, 15
Bradley, 13
Bradshaw, 15-16
Brannon, 20
Brannum, 11
Bratcher, 15
Brewer, 1, 5, 22

George, 5, 7, 20
Gerhardt, 16
Gettis, 5
Gibson, 8-9, 12-14
Gillespie, 9
Gist, 8
Glenny, 3
Godair, 8
Godby, 20
Godwin, 4, 8
Goldsmith, 3, 15
Gooch, 11, 17
Goodin, 17
Goodman, 9, 15, 19, 21
Goodrich, 10
Goodwin, 12
Gorden, 7
Gordon, 1, 16, 20
Gore, 12
Gossage, 11
Gowan, 9
Grantham, 9
Gravens, 6
Gray, 7
Green, 1, 4, 8-9, 11, 13, 21-22
Greenfield, 4, 22
Greer, 7, 9-10, 22
Gregory, 1, 13
Grey, 6
Griffin, 1, 7, 11, 13
Grigory, 5
Grimsley, 1, 7
Grissom, 15
Grogan, 4
Groomes, 15
Groves, 13
Gruggett, 3
Gulledge, 19
Gunter, 19
Gurley, 11
Guthrey, 17
Gwaltney, 18
Haas, 12
Haddon, 18

Hafford, 5
Hagges, 18
Hahn, 18
Haire, 21
Haldbreak, 14
Hall, 7, 9, 12, 14, 21-22
Ham, 5
Hamilton, 20
Hammond, 22
Hammonds, 6, 10
Hampton, 3, 7, 13, 15-16, 20-22
Hamrick, 10
Hancock, 5
Hand, 1
Hankins, 17
Hapwood, 4
Harden, 7
Hardin, 9, 18
Hardison, 22
Hardy, 11
Hargraves, 10, 16
Harlin, 4
Harman, 18, 20
Harmon, 2-3
Harp, 12
Harper, 2
Harrell, 16
Harris, 17-18, 20
Harrison, 6, 8, 15-16
Hart, 3, 6, 8-9, 13-14, 19
Hartle, 16
Hartsoe, 2
Harty, 1
Harvey, 19
Hasley, 9
Hastings, 9
Hatcher, 13
Hayes, 20
Hays, 5, 10-11, 15
Haywood, 22
Healy, 1
Hearsum, 8
Heathcutt, 1

Heere, 4
Heese, 4
Hemree, 10
Hendricks, 15
Hendrix, 13, 15, 19, 22
Hendrixson, 9
Henrell, 13
Henry, 6
Henson, 18, 20
Herrell, 8, 14, 20
Herren, 10, 18
Herrington, 11
Herrman, 9
Herron, 22
Heurell, 13
Hickerson, 8
Hicks, 1, 5, 11, 15, 19-21
Higginbotham, 3
Highlander, 18
Higlin, 8
Hilderbrand, 5
Hill, 9, 12-13
Hilton, 9
Hinesley, 3
Hinnon, 10
Hodge, 8, 18, 20
Hoffman, 8
Hogland, 15
Holder, 21
Holland, 4
Hollaway, 19
Hollifield, 2, 18
Hollister, 3
Holloway, 15
Holmes, 1, 19
Holshouser, 15
Holt, 6, 9-10
Holtzhauser, 5
Honeycutt, 11
Horn, 19
Horner, 2-3, 18
House, 2, 16
Houston, 17

Volume 14 1919-1921

Though there are very few records for colored marriages in Dunklin County, the use of col for colored does show up a few times.

GROOM	BRIDE	SOLEMNIZED
Delmer Hepslin(Heflin)	Mabel Neill	27 Jun 1919
J. H. Mackin	Lois E. Rosamond	3 Jul 1919
Sherman M. Meeks	Mrs. Inez Alliston	3 Jul 1919
Eltie Maddux	Anna McCumber	5 Jul 1919
Dee McMann	Lyleete Townley	2 Jul 1919
James Herschel Pales (Poles)	Virgie Beatrice Stewart	29 Jun 1919
Joseph W. Prance	Birdie Dee Hudson	7 Jul 1919
Orley Stiers (Stices)	Lula Wilson	28 Jun 1919
Elbert Sturgon	Lettie Jackson	8 Jul 1919
S. J. Sparks	Mrs. Iva Bledsoe	5 Jul 1919
Richard Vanover	Nora Acree	5 Jul 1919
Roy Wesley	Carrye Bradley	29 Jun 1919
Charlie Walls	Bertha Wilson	5 Jul 1919
Joe B. Crews	Mrs. Ruth Parrett	16 Jul 1919
Arlie Betticks	Minnie James	19 Jul 1919
Robert Davidson	Dovie Shipley	13 Jul 1919
J. C. Davidson	Lellar Kinchen	12 Jul 1919
N. E. Gibson	Emma Hart	12 Jul 1919
John D. Jackson	Mrs. Beulah Parsons	7 Jul 1919
Guy Kinsey	Mabel Purman	28 Jun 1919
J. E. Masters	Emma Rhoden	12 Jul 1919
William Null	Carrie Kent	12 Jul 1919
Roscoe Skidmore	Kittie Cox	19 Jul 1919
J. H. Smith	Dollie Brashers	17 Jul 1919
John M. Small	Minnie Webb	3 Jul 1919
H. C. Johnson	Mrs. Bell Binkley	28 Jul 1919
H. A. Phillips	Dorris Harris	27 Jul 1919
Elmer Williams	Annie Ballard	1 Aug 1919
Benton Greenway	Mrs. Nellie Lasswell	28 Jul 1919
W. J. Allen	Dotsie Campbell	28 Jul 1919
George Eakins	Daisy Thomas	26 Jul 1919
Louie Hodge	Dossie Whitlock	30 Jul 1919
Charley Alsup	Vilena Moore	27 Jul 1919
Miles Starnes	Eunice Boyd	21 Jul 1919
Olin O. McFarland	Jelia D. Watson	2 Aug 1919

GROOM	BRIDE	SOLEMNIZED
Fate Bradshaw	Mrs. Delsie Burnes	21 Jul 1919
Charley D. Sanson	Maudie May Birckett	22 Jul 1919
Joe Story	Callie Grammer	26 Jul 1919
R. E. Rhyne	Ruth Dallors	19 Jul 1919
Eugene Nails	Mattie Ray	27 Jul 1919
Willie E. Coy	Gertie Brown	20 Jul 1919
J. A. Carter	Ellen Harris	22 Jul 1919
Arthur Vaughn	Eva Bishop	31 Jul 1919
Leonard Greenlee	Bertha Carson	2 Aug 1919
T. G. Stanfill	Mrs. Lizzie Woodall	19 Jul 1919
Couda Bird	Gertie Province	3 Aug 1919
James Tackeberry	Cora Baker	1 Aug 1919
S. D. Whitson	Elizabeth Miller	6 Aug 1919
Henry Lawson	Bessie Scott	11 Aug 1919
Alvin Pettey	Mrs. Allie Harp	27 Jul 1919
R. L. Garner	Mrs. Ella Milburn	10 Aug 1919
H. J. Rainey	Mary Maddox	12 Aug 1919
C. F. Frederickson	Leona Evans	11 Aug 1919
Rufe Miller	Maudie Bell Mann	10 Aug 1919
S. R. Graham	Dollie Cashdollar	10 Aug 1919
Ray Price	Velma Akers	14 Aug 1919
Arther B. Cawfill	Mrs. Francis V. Huff	14 Aug 1919
Arl Roberts	Lula Grubbs	14 Aug 1919
Fred Marchbanks	Nillie Low	10 Aug 1919
Shelix O. Watson	Iva Elliott	14 Aug 1919
Thomas J. Mumford	Mabel Benbrooks	3 Aug 1919
Freeman M. Creed	Bertha G. Neely	19 Aug 1919
S. L. Cruder	Mrs. Ida Samuel	18 Aug 1919
B. F. Welty	Maggie Cash	14 Aug 1919
Ed Benson	Etta Jackson	18 Aug 1919
Claude W. Mitchell	Maudie Oliver	19 Aug 1919
Geo. Mime	Mrs. Lena Sanders	19 Aug 1919
A. E. Younger	Eulah Miller	21 Aug 1919
Fred F. Harkey	Beulah Hargrove	21 Aug 1919
Will Farris	Hattie Sadler	23 Aug 1919
Grant Wilson	Carrie Willoughby	31 Aug 1919
P. A. Howard	Mrs. Nesppie Merideth	28 Aug 1919
J. A. Roden	Mrs. Margaret Hargrove	29 Aug 1919
W. H. Turner	Rilly Moss	23 Aug 1919
Thomas Travillion	Ellen Lattie	22 Aug 1919
C. A. Dowdy	Beulah Wilson	22 Aug 1919
Eure Ham	Maymie Waddell	27 Aug 1919
John Morgan	Mrs. Bessie Killeman	23 Aug 1919
Arlie Russom	Mrs. Verdie Helton	24 Aug 1919

GROOM	BRIDE	SOLEMNIZED
R. J. Turpin	Lida Turnbow	23 Aug 1919
Paul Brannum	Grace Bell	23 Aug 1919
A. H. Lintzenick	Mildred Waltrip	3 Aug 1919
Ollie Yancy	Mary E. Ivy	26 Aug 1919
H. H. Penrod	Eth__ Stanley	26 Aug 1919
Frank Martin	Allie Bell Minis	27 Aug 1919
D. L. Dewall	Z. O. Cole	27 Aug 1919
Louis Kraust	Grace Fitzpatrick	28 Aug 1919
J. W. Bland	Mrs. Mary Harty (Hartz)	23 Aug 1919
Albert Pikey	Nadie Pittman	20 Aug 1919
Win Smith	Dollie Lowe	5 Sep 1919
Chas. C. Walker	Niner Huners	5 Sep 1919
Thomas Pruett	Clara Bunting	4 Sep 1919
M. F. Blades Jr.	Maggie Wood	6 Sep 1919
Will Ray	Daisy Hall	31 Aug 1919
Charley H. Mitchell	Virgie McKee	6 Sep 1919
J. W. Fuqua	Mrs. Rosa Youngblood	6 Sep 1919
Charles Bishop	Myrtle Billips	8 Sep 1919
R. H. Blair	Minnie McCullough	10 Sep 1919
Charley Wm. Cook	Pearl Zora Farmer	4 Sep 1919
Herman D. Griffin	Annie Elsworth	14 Sep 1919
J. J. Draper	Mrs. Rosie Poe	13 Sep 1919
Walter Godwin	Ruth Willoughby	15 Sep 1919
D. A. Ruffin	Charlotte Parker	15 Sep 1919
E. V. Pruett	Mrs. Lyda Wordly	17 Sep 1919
Robert Gattis	Bessie Edwards	23 Jun 1919
H. E. Clark	Sylvia A. Robinson	17 Sep 1919
Ed Williams	Rena Taber	27 Sep 1919
Larence Moren	Ora Pruiett	27 Sep 1919
Geo. Bruce	Loney Purvia	27 Sep1919
Riley Stephens	Flora Braglin	26 Sep 1919
Pride Reddick	Olla Ethel Slinkard	24 Sep 1919
H. C. Byard	Mrs. Cora C. Truitt (Pruitt)	22 Sep 1919
Isom Grimsly	Gracie Carter	22 Sep 1919
James Hamlin	Adelia McCown	22 Sep 1919
Vincent W. Tenkhoff	Kathleen Ashraft (Ashcraft)	23 Sep 1919
Charles L. Mims	Bessie Walker	20 Sep 1919
James E. Griggs	Hester May Brotherson	15 Sep 1919
Ben Southerland	Stella Kenser	10 Sep 1919
Harry George	Lulu Weaver	26 Aug 1919
John H. Herperien	Hilda M. Stratman	10 Sep 1919
Will Voss	Mrs. Daisy Williams	31 Aug 1919
Everet H. Elder	Nona Marie Larmore	4 Oct 1919
Joseph L. Blume	Edna Lanx	8 Oct 1919

GROOM	BRIDE	SOLEMNIZED
J. H. McReath	Ida Robertson	10 Oct 1919
Wallace Tanner	Alzada Williams	8 Oct 1919
Ernest Gulledge	Grace Mitchell	9 Oct 1919
A. H. Moyer	Mrs. Nellie Owen	7 Oct 1919
Hartwell Shaffer	Thelma Hester	6 Oct 1919
Ealey Burton	Ora Smith	5 Oct 1919
Grant Berry	Ella Baker	4 Oct 1919
Albert A. Wikowsky	Lilliam Tachings (Gachings)	4 Oct 1919
Tom Dairl	Mrs. Bertha Stricklin	4 Oct 1919
Oris Hanks	Mrs. Lillie Dunklin	4 Oct 1919
Clay Hammons	Thelma Stewart	3 Oct 1919
Leslie Deason	Bertha Morris	5 Oct 1919
F. G. Sims	Rosie Romines	1 Oct 1919
Dewey Ridings	Willie Shands	28 Sep 1919
Arthur Miller	Allie Gromer	30 Sep 1919
John Eaton	Lectie Boyles	30 Sep 1919
Ardell Willoughby	Edna Gamble	30 Sep 1919
C. W. Matthews	Mrs. Dora Bagby	11 Oct 1919
T. R. Meek	Mattie Burkhart	12 Nov 1919
Obed Noeuell	Pearl Wagster	1 Nov 1919
J. H. Preslar	Elsie Myers	1 Nov 1919
Fred H. Cloud	Allishia McElyea	12 Oct 1919
Bryon Palmer	Bertha Hall	10 Nov 1919
Claud Moxley	Reba McDonold	8 Nov 1919
Harry Day	Lucile McElerath	8 Nov 1919
Lee Murphy	Cora Baker	8 Nov 1919
Edward Graham	Maggie Back	10 Nov 1919
Joe Clark	Mrs. Minnie Wolear	10 Nov 1919
Clint Busby	Sylvia Jones	23 Oct 1919
(Mrs.) F. G. Kraft	Eula Finney	4 Oct 1919
Chas. O. Neuell	Lena Lyles	11 Oct 1919
Oscar Meadows	Lillian Bradsher	16 Oct 1919
Frank J. Schultze	Lela Mattingly	21 Oct 1919
John Steward	Mattie May Herrell	15 Oct 1919
Victor J. Thiesmann	Estelle M. C. Frisch	28 Oct 1919
Ernest Crawley	Rosa Riney	19 Oct 1919
Geo. Huggins	Mabe Brydon	17 Oct 1919
Jean Havill	Delola Glascoe	17 Oct 1919
Cecil C. Turberville	Beulah Stephens	18 Oct 1919
Lee R. Kittrell	Tessie Bowman	26 Oct 1919
Claude Mason	Etta Talley	22 Oct 1919
Walter McCumber	Nettye Lester	21 Oct 1919
Ernest Surber	Esuria Gooch	22 Oct 1919
J. M. Robertson	Gertrude Berry	22 Oct 1919

GROOM	BRIDE	SOLEMNIZED
Garland Brown	Nina Battles	24 Oct 1919
Otis Simpkins	Georgia Kelly	25 Oct 1919
Homer Sims	Paralee Tanner	26 Oct 1919
Orlie Ross	Vernie Mitchell	26 Oct 1919
John Strephens	Adie Snider	26 Oct 1919
Columbus Richardson	Rader Dunivan	27 Oct 1919
John Thraser	Jennie Snider	1 Nov 1919
Oliver Barnett	Nellie Weaver	1 Nov 1919
Clyde Green	Beulah Hartsol (Hartsoe)	17 Oct 1919
J. A. Griffin	Lula Bailey	21 Oct 1919
J. W. Norris	Ola E. Owens	17 Oct 1919
Thomas Lemonds	Mamie Myrick	16 Nov 1919
Dave Nelson	Effie Morgan	17 Nov 1919
John G. Sheer	Verna Lee	20 Nov 1919
John Bridgeman	Iva Beggs	22 Nov 1919
Raymond Davidson	Ada McFarlin	16 Nov 1919
J. M. Thorn	Myrna Vancil	25 Nov 1919
Louis Brannum	Ella Bell Smith	22 Nov 1919
Walter E. Gould	Alena May Hogg	9 Nov 1919
Harvey Denam	Macey Ezell	8 Nov 1919
Alvis Bruce	Allice Amick	29 Nov 1919
Dale Perkins	Mauriel Parker	23 Nov 1919
R. E. Lizenbee	Addie Sack	26 Nov 1919
J. H. Bledsoe	Anna Jardan	28 Nov 1919
William Wells	Lizzie Walker	12 Nov 1919
John Halley	Nettie Taylor	14 Nov 1919
N. L. Hartsoe (Hartsol)	Shelly Reagan	14 Nov 1919
Lenard Sackman	Mrs. Mable Mables	19 Nov 1919
Joseph Stenger	Elsie Meyer	26 Nov 1919
J. E. Masters	Altha Berry	19 Nov 1919
James S. Vincent	Eva L. King	22 Nov 1919
Ervin Clarey	Alice Barnett	22 Nov 1919
James L. Brown	Belle Northington	1 Dec 1919
Kinley Vincent	Alice Burch	1 Dec 1919
Dewey Sandefur	Lala Dublin	22 Nov 1919
Boyd Smith	Stella Jones	14 Dec 1919
Aleck Hartle	Mattie Johnson	1 Dec 1919
Harry Gardner	Ethel Green	30 Nov 1919
Edna _ Arley	Lucinda Westmoreland	16 Dec 1919
Howard Wynn	Agness Redding	14 Dec 1919
George Ollerman	Eva Meek	31 Nov 1919
Samuel R. Rodgers	Meada M. Morgan	16 Dec 1919
Roy Harrison	Myrtle Bailey	14 Dec 1919
John _. Wimberley	Susan A. Pitts	13 Dec 1919

GROOM	BRIDE	SOLEMNIZED
Ulysses McConnell	Lula Usry	9 Dec 1919
James H. Blader	Mrs. Dixie Hawkins	16 Dec 1919
James Lee Hollinseed	Annie Lois Briggs	8 Dec 1919
Frank W. Speed	Sarah Allen	10 Dec 1919
Geo. G. Joines	Dora Turner	2 Dec 1919
T. R. Kirk	Mrs. Lunetty Collins	7 Dec 1919
Claude McMorris	Rheo Tibbetts	10 Dec 1919
Franklin Beggs	Annie Daias	14 Dec 1919
Pearl Walker	Nancy Furgeson	17 Dec 1919
Clarence H. Snider	Edith Allen	17 Dec 1919
Sam Tucker	Stillie Moore	13 Dec 1919
Rollie Wickersham	Irene Avery	20 Dec 1919
Laurence Bass	Macel Maddox	20 Dec 1919
Geo. W. Trout	Chloe Riggs	21 Dec 1919
Riley Capps	Laura Gordin	23 Dec 1919
Fred L. Meadows	Gustie Hays	24 Dec 1919
Jasper Swiney	Dena Lowry	25 Dec 1919
Morving Ewing	Mable Craig	23 Dec 1919
A. V. White	Thelma Vaughn	24 Dec 1919
A. L. Kennedy	Lillie Letna	25 Dec 1919
Emmitt Sutton	Bernie Cook	26 Dec 1919
Elmer Collins	Bessie Aldridge	26 Dec 1919
Geo. W. Baker	Pearl Biggs	28 Dec 1919
J. B. Brotherton	Dixie Lebo	4 Jan 1920
Foley Harkey	Mamie Sanford	4 Jan 1920
Clyde M. Frye	Pauline Sardo (Sando)	4 Jan 1920
_. E. Bodine	Florence Marler	3 Jan 1920
C. A. Mount	Partena Marlor	2 Jan 1920
Conway Vaughn	Cora May Stout	4 Jan 1920
Anson Courter	Opal Gibson	23 Dec 1919
Louis J. Trail	Clara Johnson	28 Dec 1919
Justus Brewer	Aquilla Bruce	28 Dec 1919
Jess Herndon	Ola Waltman	1 Jan 1920
Elick Mitchell (col)	Blanche Hale (col)	31 Dec 1919
Roy Milam	Martha Childress	27 Dec 1919
Samuel D. Masterson	Lenora Welteck	26 Dec 1919
Houston Wilkerson	Hazel V. Sutton	24 Dec 1919
Ora Karnes	Dovie Collins	21 Nov 1919
Lem Wingate	Nora Austin	29 Dec 1919
Alex Brimager	Limma Muse	19 Dec 1919
John W. Masters	Odessie A. Shands	28 Dec 1919
Robert B. Luckett	Gladys Wright	3 Jan 1920
Louis Wiegand	Marcella Stratman	14 Jan 1920
John Wallace	Stella Neal	4 Jan 1920

GROOM	BRIDE	SOLEMNIZED
Hiram Parish	Pearl Huffstutler	4 Jan 1920
Claud L. Lester	Lillean Hickerson	7 Jan 1920
Hermill Miller	Octavo Whitler	9 Jan 1920
Dan Lacewell	Mrs. Francis Lay	11 Jan 1920
Dewey Green	Veda Houchen	10 Jan 1920
Emil P. Hargraves	May Willis	10 Jan 1920
Geo. Wakefield	Florence Lomax	14 Jan 1920
E. H. Reese	Levada Petty	15 Jan 1920
Luther Heflin	Izora Thompson	16 Jan 1920
Tom Aldridge	Hellen Huddleston	31 Jan 1920
William O. Williford	Nellie Brimager	15 Jan 1920
Jessie Swindle	Delia Bilderback	14 Jan 1920
William D. James	Frohna Whitaker	17 Jan 1920
J. N. Dillen	Ruth Hedgepeth	15 Jan 1920
William A. Hembree	Genette Trenary	16 Jan 1920
Sammie Stamps	Gracie Turner	24 Jan 1920
Claude Perry	Inez Rodgers	25 Jan 1920
T. K. Williams	Henrietta Waltrip	27 Jan 1920
J. W. Ledbetter	Martha E. Edmunson	26 Jan 1920
Erire Kembrow	Ollie Maclun	31 Jan 1920
Bert Westmoreland	Mrs. Annie Grissom	28 Jan 1920
Bellry Horn	Pearl McGrew	29 Jan 1920
Vasten R. Harden	Willie Ranes	29 Jan 1920
Arthur Roland	Lilly Jones	3 Feb 1920
Chester Hollock	Clara McCord	31 Jan 1920
Leo Sando	Lucy Hutchins	4 Feb 1920
J. W. Gunn	Ella Edwards	5 Feb 1920
G. C. Walker	Londa Staples	5 Feb 1920
Robert Hall	Mrs. Lenora Gambold	8 Feb 1920
Oscar Lacey	Bessie Mosley	7 Feb 1920
Elmer Taylor	Lois Lynch	6 Feb 1920
Don Shepard	Mayme Eakins	6 Feb 1920
Eddie Capps	Flora Harrison	7 Feb 1920
Luther Frey	Effie Sansom	7 Feb 1920
Edwin S. Hall	Velma Skidmore	7 Feb 1920
Broughton Henderson	Nina Davis	22 Nov 1919
Virgil Schrull	Myrtle Goodman	5 Dec 1919
Orville Zimmerman	Adah G. Hemphill	18 Dec 1919
Arthur Car (Cox)	Gertrude Boss	7 Feb 1920
Dix Winstar	Maude Bradsher	24 Feb 1920
Lee Warren	Parazetta Stattler	11 Feb 1920
Marlin Shipman	Eva M. Waddell	11 Feb 1920
Olen Pleasant	Ruby Ogden	12 Fcb 1920
Elva E. McConnell	Gertrude Markle	12 Feb 1290

GROOM	BRIDE	SOLEMNIZED
Harry Nunnery	Cordelia Rodgers	12 Feb 1920
A. J. Shaw	Ardona Musgrove	11 Feb 1920
Robert F. Adams	Nell Bannister	13 Feb 1920
Charles Grimes	Lossie Higginbotham	15 Feb 1920
Paul A. Shields	Gladys Walsh	21 Feb 1920
H. T. Winberry	Audrey Wilson	18 Feb 1920
Frank H. Jarman	Mayme Temples	18 Feb 1920
C. T. Green	Mrs. Elfey Young	18 Feb 1920
Claude Jones	Eltha Thurmond	22 Feb 1920
S. Frank Robinson	Mary Elizabeth Norton	27 Feb 1920
Ed Austin	Lillie Miles	22 Feb 1920
R. M. Blaylock	Nina E. Whitaker	25 Fed 1920
F. L. Keowen	Mrs. M. M. Neely	24 Feb 1920
James F. Williams	Sarah May Smart	25 Feb 1920
W. B. Solomon	Nannie Poplin	25 Feb 1920
Sam Henson	Minnie Millen	26 Feb 1920
Walter Robertson	Lora Hunt	29 Feb 1920
Robert Davis	Mrs. Pie Huff	2 Mar 1920
Sylvester Jones	Ida May Cook	3 Mar 1920
Herman White	Clarie V. Thomas	30 Mar 1920
John Hendricks	Eva Rock	20 Mar 1920
Dave Robinson	Ethel Williams	22 Mar 1920
Ed Causey	Mrs. Rosella Williams	13 Mar 1920
Frank Brigman	Rosa Wright	12 Mar 1920
Sidney C. Davis	Vergie Taylor	13 Mar 1920
H. C. Matt	Mrs. Maggie McDowell	26 Mar 1920
Sam Smith	Myrtle Sutherlin	24 Mar 1920
W. B. Thornbrough	Lillie Baty (Batz)	21 Mar 1920
Fred Fisher	Sarah Marks	1 Mar 1920
Johnny Hobbs	Bert Wilkey	13 Mar 1920
Oscar Lee Hayden	Mae Scott	28 Feb 1920
J. E. Riding	Evaline King	7 Mar 1920
Aurthor Kirby	Tina Robertson	6 Mar 1920
Omer E. Hall	Pauline Whittwick	6 Mar 1920
G. W. Pruett	Arie Davis	15 Feb 1920
D. C. Merideith	Edna Bridwell	10 Mar 1920
I. J. Carter	Jola O'dell	22 Feb 1920
Gilbert T. Bowers	Etta May McElyea	12 Mar 1920
T. J. Osborn	Mrs. Maggie Keely	25 Mar 1920
Will Esters	Emma Cowans	27 Mar 1920
Charlie Goldsmith	Flora Emery	5 Apr 1920
Charles Edmonson	Callie Eden	5 Apr 1920
John Wheeler	Mrs. Rosa Rector	3 Apr 1920
John L. Sando	Dora G. Hooper	7 Feb 1920

GROOM	BRIDE	SOLEMNIZED
Walter Tucker	Nellie Gray	2 Apr 1920
Lee Edmunds	Bertha V. Rust	3 Apr 1920
Dewey Philhower	Elsie James	3 Apr 1920
Louis Shaver	Hazel Maples	5 Apr 1920
Isaac Lyons	Pearl Belt	30 Mar 1920
Earl Beck	Azla Winters	4 Apr 1920
W. A. (Dock) Pelts	Ruth Hargroves	8 Apr 1920
John Matheny	Leota Thornton	15 Apr 1920
Everett Kinder	Sylva Maddox	14 Apr 1920
Milburn D. Clark	Lillie Vaughn	4 Apr 1920
Joe Carlyle	Birdella Ladd	10 Apr 1920
Henry E. Nations	Gracie M. Markle	4 Apr 1920
Daniel W. Thornberry	Maude L. Brooks	10 Apr 1920
Grover C. Cleary	Eula C. Horn	2 Apr 1920
Clyde Lunsford	Julia Masterson	13 Apr 1920
Leslie L. Olson	Rose M. Walker	14 Apr 1920
Curtis Moore	Hettie Damron	7 Apr 1920
R. W. Sanders	Magdaline Lynn	16 Apr 1920
William Windle	Maude May Johnson	16 Apr 1920
Rosco Paul	Oda Basinger	21 Apr 1920
W. H. Dale	Mrs. Gladys Schweikle	21 Apr 1920
J. W. Denton	U. R. Bishop	18 Apr 1920
Marion G. Culbertson	Katie Baugher	19 Apr 1920
J. B. Cothron	Ellia Yant	10 Mar 1920
John Richardson	Etta Hurst	22 Apr 1920
George Browne	Ella Williams	17 Apr 1920
Will Harmon	Flora Akridge	18 Apr 1920
Sidney Aldridge	Nora McAllister	18 Apr 1920
Ed Lownsdale	Beulah Holt	23 Apr 1920
C. E. Beck	Maggie Maslon (Marlon)	23 Apr 1920
J. H. Gaston	Mary Parker	24 Apr 1920
Frank Samples	Mrs. Cinthie Asher	23 Apr 1920
Floyd Chidster	Lula Carroll	27 Apr 1920
Cecil H. Tolley	Ethel Joiner	24 Apr 1920
Marshall Smith	Lela Joiner	24 Apr 1920
William Beauford	Gracie Hardin	23 Apr 1920
Pearl Smith	Pearl Lockard	28 Apr 1920
Chris Wright	Edna Sargent	27 Apr 1920
Arthur T. Sale	Virgie L. Parson	3 May 1920
Samuel W. Wayne	Ethel Morgan	2 May 1920
James Cagle	Eva Lee Collins	6 Mar 1920
John Gains	Dollie Bryant	23 May 1920
Thomas P. Neill	Bessie Skipper	23 May 1920
Walton Slaughter	Gealie McNeal	23 May 1920

GROOM	BRIDE	SOLEMNIZED
P. T. Tuck	Fronia Williams	22 May 1920
Otis Mabery	Gracie Victoria Hixson	16 May 1920
Bryan Wilburn	Nellie Dean	15 May 1920
A. J. Kerfoot	Myrtle Maye McAlexander	18 May 1920
Frank Gray	Mary Overall	20 May 1920
Jim Rogers	Ora Hoxworth	12 May 1920
O. B. Harris	Mary L. Kitchen	19 May 1920
F. P. Blanchard	Ida Bell Halsey	6 May 1920
W. B. Revelle	Nettie May Ledbetter	16 Mar 1920
Pearl Englehardt	Rosa Walker	25 May 1920
Albert Jones	Maude Carmack	13 May 1920
Luther Graf	Nora Rushin	15 May 1920
Claude McGill	Lenora Hatfield	17 May 1920
Arther T. Sale	Virdie L. Parson	3 May 1920
Repeat entry		
Alvin J. Kranke	Rita L. Ross	26 May 1920
Earl G. Finney	Hettie Belle McMunn	10 Apr 1920
Edward Jones	Effie S. McFarland	22 May 1920
John Legan (Logan)	Edith Blackburn	2 Apr 1920
Otto Summers	Rosa M. Wagner	22 May 1920
Max Damron	Virta Marler	6 May 1920
Jessie Hicks	Mae Braud	2 May 1920
William B. Lamb	Ella May Jones	21 Apr 1920
John Peters	Alma Knapf	5 May 1920
Lester F. Smith	Mrs. Bertha Berger	2 May 1920
Lilbert Wheeler	Bettie Rogers	2 May 1920
La Clede Waters (col)	Virginia Duffy (col)	6 May 1920
William Watson	Harriet Bodine	31 May 1920
Ralph E. Scantlands	Lela Johnson	3 Jun 1920
Albert H. Thomas	Minnie Walls	7 Jun 1920
Elmer French	Eula Owens	20 Jun 1920
Louis A. Waters	Geneva E. Wagner	20 Jun 1920
Earl Green	Ellie Rideout	22 Jun 1920
Felix Greenwell	Mrs. Bertha Skinner	19 Jun 1920
Johnnie Crafton	Carrie Holt	5 Jun 1920
Thomas M. Dugger	Mrs. Clara Preasler	7 Jun 1920
Charles H. Bailey	Mrs. Alma Speakman	30 Jun 1920
Presly R. Smith	Birdie McWherter	11 May 1920
Ira Rickman	Clara Stafford	1 Jul 1920
Ray Thorpe	Maudy Easley	30 Jun 1920
Monroe Sissom	Mary Virgin Price	6 Jun 1920
Edd Dismukes	Naomi Vowell	5 Jul 1920
Albert Palmer	Cora Handley	22 Jun 1920
J. W. Baird	Zora Hayes	22 Jun 1920

GROOM	BRIDE	SOLEMNIZED
Charley Goines	Mrs. Ollie Medley	25 Jun 1920
Pierce Duncan	Mrs. Melissa Brards	26 Jun 1920
Robert R. Kegley	Mrs. Lona Gore	27 Jun 1920
Joe A. Husteci	Mrs. Bessie Kennedy	26 Jun 1920
Homer George	Sadie Miner	26 Jun 1920
C. P. Carpenter	Mrs. Elizabeth Oliver	26 Jun 1920
Jess L. Dudley	Pearl Hills	28 Jun 1920
Charles H. Walls	Lillie May Heath	26 Jun 1920
Floyd Polan	Lena Batz (Baty)	29 Jun 1920
Earl King	Minnie Keathley	29 Jun 1920
Clyde McGill	Pearl Moore	12 Jun 1920
Oscar L. Mitchell	Elsie L. Smith	12 Jun 1920
Roy L. Stanley	Ada Abshire	16 Jun 1920
Elmer George	Mrs. Maggie Swiner	14 Jun 1920
Alvin Redman	Leora Huggins	12 Jun 1920
John C. Hendrix	Mrs. Carrie Holt	7 Jun 1920
John H. Harvel	Ma_on Miller	13 May 1920
Dewey Harrolds	Lora Lemonds	22 May 1920
Jim Brimager	Pearl Lack	23 May 1920
Johnie Bard	Rosa Lovins	12 Jun 1920
John Underwood	Effie Sedrist	8 Jun 1920
Ralph Shelton	Myrtle Wooleene	13 Jun 1920
James Ernest Sharp	Ibbie Irene Napper	8 Jun 1920
Audlee Fletcher	Ellen McNees	4 Jul 1920
Chas. Atlee Green	Ouida S. Blair	2 Jul 1920
Dewer Morrison	Nellie Smith	22 Jul 1920
John Clubb	Lena Jackson	7 Aug 1920
M. C. Weaks	Della Musgrove	2 Aug 1920
Roy C. Fleck	Mres. Ida Burness	17 Aug 1920
Elmer Dunscomb	Retta James	4 Aug 1920
Flin White	Lorla Campbell	2 Aug 1920
Charles W. Brown	Corrine F. O'Brien	5 Aug 1920
Jacob Cameron Lincoln	Dottie I. Green	2 Aug 1920
Foster Weaver	Bertha Pruett	6 Aug 1920
E. E. Carnal	Maggie Griffin	29 Jul 1920
Charles Green	Margaret Hietz	4 Aug 1920
W. A. Holder	Mrs. Kate Toliver	12 Aug 1920
G. W. Davis	Mrs. Zora Cook	22 Jul 1920
J. W. Durbin	Levina Jones	15 Aug 1920
William A. Brown	Susie Heath	14 Aug 1920
A. S. Milam	Mrs. Annie Pierson	1 Aug 1920
Francis Abare	Ether Forrets	15 Aug 1920
G. B. Staggs	Mrs. Eva Mettison	25 Aug 1920
Albert A. Abbey	Maude McGill	22 Aug 1920

GROOM	BRIDE	SOLEMNIZED
Ed McCuen	Mrs. Lottie Frye	23 Aug 1920
George Jones	Mrs. May Yarbrough	20 Aug 1920
Frank Ford	Lillie Pugh	22 Aug 1920
Abraham Perkins	Eva C. Briggs	28 Aug 1920
James Estes	Veda McIllwain	30 Aug 1920
Hary Jackson	Notria Brown	30 Aug 1920
Walter Disher	Lucil Hodges	7 Aug 1920
Albert Mullinex	Clara Patterson	8 Aug 1920
Gil ford Johnson	Estella Jones	2 Aug 1920
L. W. Kirkwood	Luron Walker	8 Aug 1920
Bluford Grice	Bonnie Wood	7 Aug 1920
Alferd Starnes	Maudie Surnney	21 Aug 1920
Lovell Stuart	Rosie Byrd	19 Aug 1920
H. J. Morgan	Ella Cowan	7 Aug 1920
Bonnie Boone	Esthel Jones	17 Aug 1920
Henry Hunter	Mrs. Mary Cox	31 Jul 1920
George Dickie	Ada Winters	31 Jul 1920
Buster Ellis	Mrs. Drue Kruse	14 Jul 1920
John Joseph	Alice Lewis	28 Jul 1920
Beckham Southern	Mary Edna Houston	20 Jul 1920
J. W. Caldwell	Mrs. Ada Meadows	24 Jul 1920
William H. Mcgrew	Zelma L. Linen	22 Jull 1920
W. R. Myers	Mrs. Hilda Davis	30 May 1920
William Henry McMahan	Allice Morgan	25 Jul 1920
Goldie Nash	Lottie Davison	15 Jul 1920
Joseph G. Gordon	Lillie Masterson	18 Jul 1920
Chas. Damson	Daisy Wyrick	14 Jul 1920
Albert M. Wicker	Kate Marshall	21 Jul 1920
Clarence Bradshaw	Stella Cashdollar	23 Jun 1920
Henry Lankford	Lora Morgan	11 Jul 1920
Charlie Bassett	Emma Ray	2 Jul 1920
Rosmus Blackman	Nettie Vineyard	4 Jul 1920
Loyd Mangold	Lela Anderson	13 Jul 1920
H. W. Martin	Mrs. Dollie Cross	13 Aug 1920
Roy Dickerson	Virgie Jordan	20 Aug 1920
Birt Boone	Irene McIlvoy	21 Aug 1920
Willie Moss	Orfina L. Snider	7 Jul 1920
Clyde Wright	Letha McFarland	24 Aug 1920
James Moss	Mrs. Alice Pierson	24 Aug 1920
Ross Abernathy	Marie Wilson	25 Aug 1920
William A. Pruett	Mrs. Alice Price	25 Aug 1920
L. J. Matlock	Callie Schram	27 Aug 1920
William McClain	Mrs. Laura Young	26 Jun 1920
Sammie Ledgerwood	Lucy Higgs	26 Aug 1920

GROOM	BRIDE	SOLEMNIZED
Burley Baker	Mrs. Alice C. Kirk	28 Aug 1920
Luther F. Brandon	Alice McAllister	28 Aug 1920
J. O. Craven	Mrs. Zelma Crenshaw	28 Aug 1920
George Gallemore	Luly Catto	31 Aug 1920
Charlie Williamson	Golda Sansom	31 Aug 1920
George Fortman	Matilda Ranspiez	8 Sep 1920
Bernard Siebert	Wilhelmina Fortman	8 Sep 1920
Roland A. Chambers	Mrs. Nettie Proffer	1 Sep 1920
Luther Marlow	Ethel Wellin	2 Sep 1920
Thomas D. Lasater	Mrs. Myrtle Hall	1 Sep 1920
Sidney N. Grimwood	Flora E. Snow	4 Sep 1920
Floyd McGinnis	Opal Looney	5 Sep 1920
J. P. Collins	Mrs. Rosie Howard	6 Sep 1920
Herman Blazier	Eva Bridgeman	6 Sep 1920
Lex Coy	Pearl Ayres	4 Sep 1920
Jim Pritt	Alma Lunsford	16 Aug 1920
Emmett N. Huff	Elizabeth Martin	6 Aug 1920
Charlie Moris	Cinthia Gilbert	29 Aug 1920
James E. Holder	Bertha L. Fuller	10 Jul 1920
G. C. Solesbee	Mildred M. Brockman	5 Jun 1920
Edward Boner	Mrs. Lula Hodge	26 Aug 1920
Earnest Gromer	Addie Masbre	19 Sep 1920
Will Johnston	Meady Carr	14 Sep 1920
Shelby C. Godsey	Lilliam Agnes James	9 Sep 1920
Roman Maples	Millard Laster	13 Sep 1920
Floyd Vernon	Pearl Sample	14 Sep 1920
Rurby Bowman	Bertha Brown	14 Sep 1920
Lee J. Wells	Myrtle Husband	19 Sep 1920
W. S. Wimberley	Gertie Stones	11 Sep 1920
Ollie Derryberry	Mrs. Jova Henson	25 Sep 1920
J. W. Steward	Mrs. Mattie Arnold	16 Sep 1920
Sam Maples	Carmoa Macgill	10 Sep 1920
H. B. Hall	Yernie Pruett	11 Sep 1920
Clarance Berry	Beulah Stonecipher	11 Sep 1920
J. C. Davis	Mary Carter	18 Sep 1920
B. F. Crawford	Mattie Hartle	21 Sep 1920
N. T. Cantrell	Marie Nations	25 Sep 1920
Howell H. Clark	Millie Davis	26 Sep 1920
Charley Deken	Teresa Peters	22 Sep 1920
Alonzo L. Freeman	Tellie E. Moore	23 Sep 1920
Jewell Harris	Naelye Kennett	19 Sep 1920
Charlie Stewart	Audrey Huff	25 Sep 1920
Marion Wren (col)	Rosie Gooch (col)	Date Not Shown
Jack W. Williams	Mrs. Sallie Conrad	2 Oct 1920

GROOM	BRIDE	SOLEMNIZED
Jim Ward	Flossie Anderson	13 Jun 1920
W. J. Tatum	Bessie Riggs	2 Oct 1920
Rayburn Spence	Florence Bishop	3 Oct 1920
George Sheppard	Valeria Snyder	26 Oct 1920
Leland M. Mathis	May Williams	18 Jul 1920
Walter Henson	Willie Penny	10 Jul 1920
Tom Sides	Lottie Patterson	7 Oct 1920
H. R. Standfield	Mamie Fine	4 Oct 1920
James Gibson	Mrs. Tildie Pruitt	30 Sep 1920
Dolph G. Elliottt	Oma Sparks	7 Oct 1920
Oliver Braden	Mrs. Veleta Sanders	4 Oct 1920
Clavert D. Sutton	Letha Bechtel	8 Oct 1920
Jack C. Weiss	Mrs. Lenora Hudson	9 Oct 1920
Dan Watkins	Bertha Jones	3 Oct 1920
Isona Rogers	Janie White	8 Oct 1920
Will McNair	Dora Cashion	7 Oct 1920
Robert L. Gambling	Eathel Redman	9 Oct 1920
E. Close	Margaret Clark	7 Oct 1920
G. L. Sarver	Mrs. Ruth L. Marlin	18 Aug 1920
Dennis G. Rainey	Helen Wilson	9 Oct 1920
Finis McGarrity	Dovie Thompson	7 Oct 1920
George W. Furgeson	Beatrress Brown	8 Aug 1920
Cecil Blair	Lola Solomon	26 Aug 1920
Zack Hastings	Beatrice Hays	9 Oct 1920
Gusty Busby	Bessie Daugherty	10 Oct 1920
S. D. Biggs	Mabel Pigman (Trigman)	9 Oct 1920
Colas Bollinger	Delphia Miller	9 Oct 1920
John Anderson	Weltha McKey	10 Oct 1920
Thomas E. Crawford	Mrs. Mouttie L. Jordan	8 Sep 1920
Hugh R. Cawthon	Pearl Robertson	30 Sep 1920
Jeff Sinclair	Margrett Kiser	17 Oct 1920
H. L. Fine	Viola Clark	21 Oct 1920
M. H. Nordman	Margrett Hendricks	7 Oct 1920
Carl Ray	Dora Harp	31 Oct 1920
Rev. R. M. Onby	Mrs. Sarah Hicks	17 Oct 1920
Joe Wilson	Helen C. Goldsmith	18 Oct 1920
Robert Stroupe	Nellie Mattice	19 Oct 1920
T. L. Joiner	Mrs. Belle Pruett	14 Oct 1920
Herman Followell	Bertha Stephens	16 Oct 1920
N. S. Alberson	Mrs. Bertie Coffle	7 Nov 1920
Robert Adkins	Ethel Byers	23 Oct 1920
Aaron M. Binkley	Nora Lyons	7 Nov 1920
Emerson Billington	Ruby Juanita Manius	23 Nov 1920
W. E. Bittle	Myrtle Baty	1 Oct 1920

GROOM	BRIDE	SOLEMNIZED
Henry Boswell	Golda Goode	10 Nov 1920
Hubert Brydon	Stella Keele	3 Dec 1920
D. A. Brewer	Mrs. Vonie Poe	27 Nov 1920
James A. Birmingham	Ida M. Sagel	24 Nov 1920
A. J. Barnett	Lona Conyers	27 Oct 1920
Guy L. Barnett	Dora Byrd	23 Oct 1920
Herman Cato	Ida Goodwin	1 Nov 1920
Fred Cooper	Eva Armstrong	14 Nov 1920
George Washington Connor	Verby Vivian Markham	23 Nov 1920
Huston Champ	Lena Waltrip	27 Nov 1920
M. B. Dockins	Ida Rerigan (Perigan)	27 Nov 1920
John Eberhardt	Catherine Kuper	10 Nov 1920
Vernard Evans	Lena Trout	8 Nov 1920
Herbert Edmonson	Emma Swiney	7 Nov 1920
William J. Edwards	Ethel Beard	4 Nov 1920
W. C. Fain	Carrie Goza	18 Nov 1920
J. A. Drew	Jennie Ferry	16 Oct 1920
Fred Griffin	Ruth Menneke	23 Oct 1920
Fred Howlett	Mrs. Belle Crabtree	29 Nov 1920
Ben Hodges	Lucile Ratton	15 Nov 1920
Elbert Howard	Carletta King	7 Nov 1920
J. G. Moncure	Viola Wilbanks	18 Nov 1920
Homer McFarland	Flossie Stearns	5 Dec 1920
Orville Nichols	Edna Grimes	7 Nov 1920
Lyman Nations	Gertrude Wall	2 Oct 1920
Calvin Prince	Nellie Welman (Welmore)	13 Nov 1920
Jim Palmer	Mrs. Myrtle Campbell	27 Nov 1920
S. W. Pirtle	Mrs. Lula Gooch	21 Nov 1920
Luther Pearson	Bessie Graham	7 Nov 1920
Fred L. Penney	Nona L. Ashcraft	23 Nov 1920
Harley C. Pearson	Effie Shipman	24 Nov 1920
Eskarce Piley (Riley)	Mrs. Lela Gulley	18 Nov 1920
R. B. Seal	Mrs. Ida Nolin	4 Nov 1920
William Obie Stclergy	Myrtle White	4 Nov 1920
Lloyd F. Tucker	Minta Long	28 Nov 1920
Grant Weathers	Dore Lee Sikes	20 Nov 1920
J. J. Whitlow	Mrs. Martha Jane Holt	19 Nov 1920
Clinton Winters	Della Bostick	6 Nov 1920
Dave Rhen (Rhew)	Ossie Franks	15 Dec 1920
Abe Campbell	Emma Baird	14 Dec 1920
George Morgan	Sarah Westbrook	11 Dec 1920
John Nipper	Daisy Henson	7 Dec 1920
Bill Garis	Sena Sadler	7 Dec 1920
Burl Eskew	Mrs. Myrtle Childs	8 Dec 1920

GROOM	BRIDE	SOLEMNIZED
Oral L. Calveri	Nola Jones	3 Dec 1920
T. W. Read	Mrs. Ada Bennett	11 Dec 1920
Arther Waltrip	Eva Millhouse	12 Dec 1920
Ralph Lux	Ruby Stady	9 Dec 1920
Hugh Higginbotham	Nola Harkey	21 Nov 1920
Floy Hall	Emma Adams	9 Dec 1920
C. H. Griffin	Mrs. Dora Pruett	16 Dec 1920
Adam Dorris	Mrs. Anna Berry	13 Dec 1920
William H. Stewart	Ida Myers	18 Dec 1920
Burl Bibb	Dicie Powell	18 Dec 1920
Samuel B. Hunt	Nelle Hoover	18 Dec 1920
Joe Wood	Mary Bailey	19 Dec 1920
Virgil L. Medling	Ethel Willard	29 Dec 1920
Russell S. Medley	Ann H. Whiteaker	22 Dec 1920
William Metheny	Etta Julian	23 Dec 1920
E. O. Masterson	Carrie Boyd	23 Dec 1920
Nathen Riggs	Letty Richardson	22 Dec 1920
Henry Steward	Bertha Bailey	22 Dec 1920
W. B. Oden	Maggie Burkett	23 Dec 1920
Henry Ralen	Binner White	23 Dec 1920
Ray Hildebrand	Icy Velma Haislip	25 Dec 1920
Dallas L. Owens	Ethel Dillard	23 Dec 1920
G. W. Parrent	Mrs. A. B. Wheatley	24 Dec 1920
D. D. Dameron	Effie George	24 Dec 1920
Clarence McWorthey	Emma Fisher	25 Dec 1920
Cecil Dunivan	Pearl Dye	27 Dec 1920
Charles E. Garrison	Mrs. Noveda Smith	29 Dec 1920
James Dunn	Ethel McIntosh	30 Dec 1920
J. J. West	Mrs. Minnie Anders	1 Jan 1921
Thomas Tilley	Maggie Brooks	29 Dec 1920
Dallas Branum	Martha Houck	29 Dec 1920
Calvin Graham	Pearl Abney	6 Jan 1921
C. H. Sneed	Delta Denton	24 Dec 1920
Ernest Griffin	Ivy George	5 Jan 1921
Elmer E. Norton	Lessie E. MaGouirk	7 Jan 1921
John Brooks	Rosa Riley	7 Jan 1921
G. G. Wilborn	Grace Jackson	11 Jan 1921
Robert Church	Dottie McGee	8 Jan 1921
Wm. Anderson	Mora Ford	11 Jan 1921
B. E. McElyea	Jennie L. Ward	15 Jan 1921
Hursel Stanfill	Grace Yarba	15 Jan 1921
Willie Dutton	May McGee	15 Jan 1921
Harry Kelems	Zella Trobaugh	16 Jan 1921
P. B. Peck(Peek)	Mrs. Rebecca Bowman	17 Jan 1921

GROOM	BRIDE	SOLEMNIZED
Edward Creece	Annie Robertson	18 Jan 1921
E. H. Glasscock	Mae Haislip	17 Jan 1921
Ernest Loyd (col)	Tinnie Davis (col)	18 Jan 1921
Leonard Ashlock	Florence Dobbins	19 Jan 1921
W. H. Mulherin	Mrs. Victoria Porter	19 Jan 1921
D. C. Morgan	Mrs. Ora White	20 Jan 1921
Pat Fitzgerald	Elzetia Rideout	20 Jan 1921
Loran Jones	Jennie Davidson	22 Jan 1921
Roy Simpkins	Ethel Rouse	22 Jan 1921
W. R. Harkey	Mrs. Ada L. George	23 Jan 1921
Chas. Timmons	Mrs. Jennie Hammonds	27 Jan 1921
Fred Rauls	Kittie Ray	26 Jan 1921
H. E. Harp (Hays)	Evie Ayers	30 Jan 1921
Thomas Jackson	Mrs. Ellen Hill	31 Jan 1921
Ruffin Boyett	Mrs. Cassie Bean	6 Feb 1921
Geo. L. Ray	Daisy Parrent	2 Feb 1921
Clyde O'Kane	Edith Looney	3 Feb 1921
M. H. Gipson	Lillie Cagle	3 Feb 1921
Lee Roy Davis	Iva Tuttle	5 Feb 1921
J. W. Goforth	Pamy Jensieran Laden	5 Feb 1921
Otis Robinson	Zelma McElrath	5 Feb 1921
D. E. Vaughn	Mrs. Nannie Smith	6 Feb 1921
Lum Sullinger	Beulah Moore	8 Feb 1921
J. T. Sanders	Viliar Cunningham	11 Feb 1921
Jess Fox	Francis Pool	11 Feb 1921
J. H. Davis	Ettie McDannel	15 Feb 1921
Fred Collins	Mrs. Vela Carry	12 Feb 1921
Robert Davenport	Linnie Rauls (Rawls)	13 Feb 1921
Charley Berry	Mary Higgins	17 Feb 1921
Milford Sanders	Marie Cates	19 Feb 1921
Dolph Sawyer	Arzonie Leretta Young	20 Feb 1921
Ray Childers	Mary McCory	20 Feb 1921
W. B. Key	Mrs. Mary Virdie Evans	27 Feb 1921
John Wagster	Ida Sanders	21 Feb 1921
Percy Williams	Mrs. L. Rogers	20 Feb 1921
Cass Blair	Mrs. Mary Mullens	26 Feb 1921
William L. Keen	Gracie Hubbard	19 Feb 1921
William Herder	Gertrude Wilson	21 Feb 1921
Charley Land	Mrs. Maggie McCoy	21 Feb 1921
Felix E. Parker	Mary Spry	23 Feb 1921
William DeMass (DeMoss)	Zola Evans	22 Feb 1921
James E. Hamilton	Ruby Qualls	25 Feb 1921
B. A. Henson	Agness Edwards	1 Mar 1921
F. I. Vaughn	Mrs. Mary Wells	26 Feb 1921

GROOM	BRIDE	SOLEMNIZED
James V. McCracken	Mrs. Mandy L. Crosland	26 Feb 1921
Geo. Dunaway	Mrs. Emma Branum	27 Feb 1921
Ray Smiley	Mrs. Rosa Snider	26 Feb 1921
Arvel Husk	Lessie Martin	1 Mar 1921
James Wesly Holland	Annie Prior Ruddick	6 Feb 1921
J. W. Boring	Maggie Pennington	28 Feb 1921
Robert S. Eskeridge	Moy Kemp	1 Mar 1921
R. O. Johnson	Meda Burton	2 Mar 1921
Ernest Moloney	Alberta Beauchump	3 Mar 1921
Roy Harman	Wilcie Thornberry	6 Mar 1921
S. F. Carpenter	Bertha Pruett	6 Mar 1921
S. F. Goodrich	Mrs. Ella Malone	5 Mar 1921
Bill Huggins	Lillie Brydon	5 Mar 1921
Clyde Myrick	Versia Staggs	5 Mar 1921
Dan Sheppard	Cora Eakins	5 Mar 1921
Curtis Petty	Hattie Mungle	6 Mar 1921
J. E. Wright	Annie Hamby	7 Mar 1921
Willie Akers	Nell Thompson	9 Mar 1921
Francis Patton	Pheba Ann Wagoner	11 Mar 1921
Claude Ray	Birdie Boyett	10 Mar 1921
Will Smith	Mrs. Versia Laxton	11 Mar 1921
Dennis M. Taylor	Grace Smith	12 Mar 1921
Geo. Wells	Mable Black	13 Mar 1921
William Redman	Lillie Holcomb	15 Mar 1921
Curt Bassett	Effie McClure	15 Mar 1921
Ossey Maples	Catherine Jamison	20 Mar 1921
Virgie Brown (col)	Marie Stevens (col)	19 Mar 1921
Chester L. Lucas	Mamie D. Smith	25 Mar 1921
Fred Clark	Lydia Moore	23 Mar 1921
W. T. Palmer	Etta Clay	23 Mar 1921
Charley Boone	Ella Parish	24 Mar 1921
Raymond Tuberville	Leota Craig	27 Mar 1921
J. T. Ingle	Mrs. R. A. Smith	24 Mar 1921
Sol Klein	Mrs. Arpha L. Kennedy	26 Mar 1921
Chas. R. Yates	Laura Couater	26 Mar 1921
R. V. Pickett	Mrs. Martha Jacksman	30 Mar 1921
Drew Thompson	Nettie Cadle	2 Apr 1921
Wesly Griffin	Maggie Burnett	2 Apr 1921
Margin Waddell	Effie McClain	3 Apr 1921
James Lane	Lela Burgess	2 Apr 1921
Estle Fish	May Trobaugh	3 Apr 1921
Ben F. Stevens	Jesse Lindsey	4 Apr 1921
J. O. Davidson	Myrtle Lee Crayne	8 Apr 1921
G. W. Bridges	Eula Stewart	9 Apr 1921

GROOM	BRIDE	SOLEMNIZED
Charley Winchester	Rosa Hawkins	9 Apr 1921
Lee Rosenberg	Florence Quertermous	12 Apr 1921
David McFarland	Gracie Hurst	13 Apr 1921
Carl Battles	Clara Causey	16 Mar 1921
Clarence E. Snider	May J. Pennington	30 Mar 1921
R. F. Snider	Alberta Vose	30 Mar 1921
Perma K. Long	Hazel Hobbs	31 Mar 1921
J. F. Wilson	Elizabeth Jones	10 Apr 1921
Hobert Williams	Katie M. Larnaurion	6 Apr 1921
Cicero Robertson	Sarah McCauley	9 Apr 1921
Marshall Oats	Eva Rhew	5 Apr 1921
Van B. Cox	Mattie Cobb	8 Apr 1921
Ignatius P. Friedman	Helen J. Vanderfeltz	27 Apr 1921
Chas. Sweager	Maude Bracken	11 Apr 1921
William H. Fowler	Hellen M. Harris	15 Apr 1921
John Williams	Beatrice Minner	14 Apr 1921
William F. Payton	Irene Cobb	15 Apr 1921
Grady McGill	Jennettie Wyant	15 Apr 1921
J. F. Jones	Ethel Jarrett	16 Apr 1921
J. V. Rice	Blanche Harkey	16 Apr 1921
Frank Landrum	Minnie Ladd	16 Apr 1921
Henry Pierce	Audra Holmes	22 Apr 1921
Willie Brown	Nettie Metcalf	23 Apr 1921
Lemmie A. Crump	Dolly Morris	23 Apr 1921
Charly Sheets	Jennie Singleton	23 Apr 1921
Oron Smith	Elsie Grogan	26 Apr 1921
Clarence A. Carrell	Mary McFarland	29 Apr 1921
Orville McCormick	Georgia Hunt	28 Apr 1921
Curtis Sissom	Geneva McNutt	29 Apr 1921
Roy McClearen	Emma Laird	29 Apr 1921
B. L. Moore	Mrs. Rosa Wells	30 Apr 1921
Johnnie Cook	Mrs. Bertha Cook	30 Apr 1921
Finis D. Cook	Laura Nincksato	30 Apr 1921
James T Millhouse	Ella Martin	30 Apr 1921
Clarence Wilson	Imon Tolley	1 May 1921
Iza Walton	Lena Williams	13 Mar 1921
Will Jones	Mattie McKelley	7 Apr 1921
D. B. Hart	Fannie Mann	24 Apr 1921
Joe Hancock	Maude Bell	1 May 1921
Claude Holly	Edith Nunnery	2 May 1921
W. A. Dennison	Mrs. Gertie Murphy	3 May 1921
Robert Roper	Mrs. Goldie Amick	3 May 1921
James H. Poe	Mrs. Bessie Grisson	5 May 1921
James R. Downing	Meradie Winchester	7 May 1921

GROOM	BRIDE	SOLEMNIZED
Jesse French	Madjiska Straign	7 May 1921
Leeman R. Hibbs	Bertha Hardin	7 May 1921
Mike Lawrence	Mrs. Leura Monroe	7 May 1921
T. J. Morgan	Ida Myrtle Gray	7 May 1921
Elbert Malloy	Vera Ray	9 May 1921
Wylie Singleton	Vina Singleton	14 May 1921
John H. Ware	Florence Brown	14 May 1921
George G. Philips	Zala Glenn	16 May 1921
Allen Bristol	Ora Bell Autry	4 Jun 1921
Herman Blazier	Eva Bridgeman	20 Jun 1921
Harry Benson	Elsie Damron	29 May1921
Robert L. Bowden	Lelia Lillian Hildebrand	9 Jun 1921
T. J. Clark	Lida Walker	15 Jun 1921
W. A. Eakins	Mrs. Martha A. Jinken	29 May 1921
Spurgeon French	Marie Gholson	11 Jun 1921
Chas. Friend	Loue May Hopkins	18 Jun 1921
Lee Finley	Irene Earp	7 May 1921
Van Hawkins	Lura (Lena) Noble	29 May 1921
Charles T. Jones	Nellie Day	1 Jun 1921
Edward J. James	Hazel McDowell	31 May 1921
M. A. Kagley	Mrs. Maggie Hawking	18 May 1921
Pete Kohl	Leora Dees	5 Jun 1921
T. L. Landerman	Mrs. Camblee Moseby	30 May 1921
Edgar Moore	Marie Kraust	18 Jun 1921
Arthur Oldham	Rachel Cullins	8 Jun 1921
Oris Painter	Gladys Clevenger	8 Jun 1921
William Rundel	Mrs. Bertha Mitchell	27 May 1921
Cleadons E. Smith	Mrs. Hazel E. Bass	12 Jun 1921
Geo. Sutliff	Mrs. Elizabeth Long	4 Jun 1921
M. J. Tillman	Mrs. Emma Hays	May 1921
Earl J. White	Monia M. Vandine (Vandive)	12 May 1921
Lige White	Myrtle Rushin	21 May 1921
Clarence Wiseman	Ella Nanney	27 May 1921
John Wade	Mrs. Ollie Smith	2 Jun 1921
Robert Young	Grace Parker	12 Jun 1921
William A. Brockman	Hazel Lee	1 Jun 1921
J. T. McIntosh	Elsie Drew	10 Jun 1921
Guy Anderson	Flora Greer	4 Jul 1921
W. F. Scott	Ersey Nunery	5 Jul 1921
Edgar Cook	Hannah E. Abraham	25 Jun 1921
Luther Miller	Florence Dees	2 Jul 1921
Ervin Walls	Tot Woodard	4 Jul 1921
Venus Johnson	Mary E. Culberson	28 Jun 1921
Walter Bredensteiner	Wilda French	25 Mar 1921

GROOM	BRIDE	SOLEMNIZED
Sammie McElyea	Imogene Richardson	18 June 1921
W. D. Hyde	N. E. Jennings	25 Jun 1921
Albert Lemonds	Dessa Neal	19 Jun 1921
John Smith	Laura Hamilton	21 Jun 1921
W. M. Ferguson	Lida Tune	24 Jun 1921
Herbert Blankenship	Flora Cross	18 Jun 1921
Otto Kirchen	Aletrus Lee	14 Jun 1921
John George Long	Beulah Harkey	26 Jun 1921
Alvas Hogan	Mrs. Martha Edwards	30 Jun 1921
Johnie Welton Johnson	Essie Elmira Standley	25 Jun 1921
Ben Daily	Lucile Burton	30 Jun 1921
J. D. Robinson	Winnie D. Roper	28 Jun 1921
Solon Herrman	Florence Gray	1 Jul 1921
Ben E. Adams	Anna M. Mitchell	5 Aug 1921
Herman Anders (Andus)	Grace Grimes	24 Jul 1921
W. F. Biby	Gusta Hager	3 Aug 1921
Willie Brantley	Cora Ethel Grimes	17 Aug 1921
Calvin Brewer	Zilla Mason	3 Jul 1921
William W. Buck	Mildred Cumings	13 Jul 1921
J. C. Buck	Louise Henslee	14 Jul 1921
A. J. Clark	Pearl Eden	14 Aug 1921
P. R. Carver	Mrs. Cynthia Ethel Edwards	29 Aug 1921
Theodore Collins	Mirtle Weedman	9 Jul 1921
W. F. Cates	Mrs. Ida Perryman	18 Jul 1921
Fred Floyd	Alma Wilson	20 Aug 1921
Chas. Hobby	Blanche Godsey	31 Jul 1921
Arthur Hobbs	Myrtle Bracken	31 Jul 1921
C. I. Holtzhouser	N. M. Reeves	19 Aug 1921
J. F. Jones	Mrs. Emma Sickles	24 Aug 1921
Chester Keller	Margaret G. Gardner	21 Jul 1921
Clyde King	Mae Poe	24 Jul 1921
Robert Lynn	Flossey Binkley	13 Aug 1921
Coy Lincoln	Bell Rogers	16 Jul 1921
S. F. Marcum	Lela Jennings	8 Aug 1921
Orvel McKinnon	DeLaney M. Jones	21 Aug 1921
Elijah McCain	Belva Swindle	16 Jul 1921
John Phillips	Alma Williams	31 Jul 1921
Fay Painter	Anna Barcraft	5 Aug 1921
Dewey Proffer	Lora Goodwin	15 Aug 1921
Rev. C. W. Patterson	Mrs. S. A. Wilson	26 Jun 1921
J. S. Reeves	Mrs. Martha Gordon	9 Aug 1921
Arthur Stroupe	Bettie Kirkman	4 Jul 1921
William Turbville	Edith Lomunion	10 Aug 1921
Francis Williams	Elsie Conran (Conrad)	30 Jul 1921

GROOM	BRIDE	SOLEMNIZED
G. W. Myrick	Mrs. Ollie Mizell	20 Aug 1921
Carl Watson	Dollie Wright	14 Jul 1921
G. T. Adams	Ollie Perkins	5 Mar 1921
John H. Montgomery	Mrs. Nancy Cockrum	6 Aug 1921
J. W. Taylor Jr.	Almeda Beck	21 Aug 1921
Acy Gunter	Inez Williford	26 Aug 1921
William Roberds	Allie Baird	30 Aug 1921
William B. Anthony	Evelyn Mullen	31 Aug 1921
Fred McKinney	Nellie Collins	2 Sep 1921
Birt Holligan	Lula Williams	8 Sep 1921
Rube Campbell	Roena Moore	10 Sep 1921
H. T. West	Mrs. Martha Mauldin	14 Sep 1921
E. R. Harris	Audry Morgan	15 Sep 1921
Joe Shands	Lena Erhardt	Date Not Shown
Earl Surber	Janie Wright	24 Sep 1921
Robert W. Edwards	Elsie George	25 Sep 1921
Hugh Buckner	Nola Welch	30 Sep 1921
John Knight	Bertha Kitrel	1 Oct 1921
Herman Williams	Dollie Watson	1 Oct 1921
Joe Wilkins	Ethel Benton	30 Sep 1921

Nordman, 45
Norris, 36
Northington, 36
Norton, 39, 47
Null, 32
Nunery, 51
Nunnery, 39, 50
O'Brien, 42
O'dell, 39
O'Kane, 48
Oats, 50
Oden, 47
Ogden, 38
Oldham, 51
Oliver, 33, 42
Ollerman, 36
Olson, 40
Onby, 45
Osborn, 39
Overall, 41
Owen, 35
Owens, 36, 41, 47
Painter, 51-52
Pales, 32
Palmer, 35, 41, 45, 49
Parish, 38, 49
Parker, 34, 36, 40, 48, 51
Parrent, 47-48
Parrett, 32
Parson, 40-41
Parsons, 32
Patterson, 43, 45, 52
Patton, 49
Paul, 40
Payton, 50
Pearson, 46
Peck, 47
Peek, 47
Pelts, 40
Penney, 46
Pennington, 49-50
Penny, 45
Penrod, 34
Perigan, 46
Perkins, 36, 43, 53

Perry, 38
Perryman, 52
Peters, 41, 44
Pettey, 33
Petty, 38, 49
Philhower, 40
Philips, 51
Phillips, 32, 52
Pickett, 49
Pierce, 50
Pierson, 42
Pigman, 45
Pikey, 34
Piley, 46
Pirtle, 46
Pittman, 34
Pitts, 36
Pleasant, 38
Poe, 34, 46, 50, 52
Polan, 42
Poles, 32
Pool, 48
Poplin, 39
Porter, 48
Powell, 47
Prance, 32
Preasler, 41
Preslar, 35
Price, 33, 41, 43
Prince, 46
Pritt, 44
Proffer, 44, 52
Province, 33
Pruett, 34, 39, 42-45, 47, 49
Pruiett, 34
Pruitt, 34, 45
Pugh, 43
Purman, 32
Purvia, 34
Qualls, 48
Quertermous, 50
Rainey, 33, 45
Ralen, 47
Ranes, 38
Ranspiez, 44

Ratton, 46
Rauls, 48
Rawls, 48
Ray, 33-34, 43, 45, 48-49, 51
Read, 47
Reagan, 36
Rector, 39
Reddick, 34
Redding, 36
Redman, 42, 45, 49
Reese, 38
Reeves, 52
Rerigan, 46
Revelle, 41
Rhen, 46
Rhew, 46, 50
Rhoden, 32
Rhyne, 33
Rice, 50
Richardson, 36, 40, 47, 52
Rickman, 41
Rideout, 41, 48
Riding, 39
Ridings, 35
Riggs, 37, 45, 47
Riley, 46-47
Riney, 35
Roberds, 53
Roberts, 33
Robertson, 35, 39, 45, 48, 50
Robinson, 34, 39, 48, 52
Rock, 39
Roden, 33
Rodgers, 36, 38-39
Rogers, 41, 45, 48, 52
Roland, 38
Romines, 35
Roper, 50, 52
Rosamond, 32
Rosenberg, 50
Ross, 36, 41
Rouse, 48

Volume 15 1921-1923

Though there are very few records for colored marriages in Dunklin County, the use of col for colored does show up a few times. There is one entry for 1920.

GROOM	BRIDE	SOLEMNIZED
Oda Reeves	Mittie Parker	1 Sep 1921
Claude Simpson	Ruby Bowman	3 Sep 1921
F. A. Barley (Bailey)	Ruth Moore	3 Sep 1921
Geo. L. Clark	Beatrice Guillory	4 Sep 1921
A.J. Bledsoe	Flora Capps	3 Sep 1921
Louis W. Birt	Dessie M. Miller	3 Sep 1921
Alvin Nunley	Ada Akers	3 Sep 1921
L. C. Coffell	Rosa Warf	6 Sep 1921
Guy E. Knight	Ethel M. Maloney	8 Sep 1921
Thomas Elsworth	Gladys Singleton	10 Sep 1921
Frank Sitz	Mrs. May Lincoln	10 Sep 1921
Gilbert Biggs	Maudy Ainley	14 Sep 1921
James E. Norris	Irene Edwards	18 Sep1 921
W.P. Griffin	Mrs. Cerelda Windberry	17 Sep 1921
Arvil Mason	Louise Chapman	1 Sep 1921
John Thomas	Idell Nations	17 Sep 1921
William Stanfill	Edith Roe	14 Sep 1921
Johnnie Robinson	Liddy Onesicha Grimes	18 Sep 1921
Marion Shans	Vivia Smith	21 Sep 1921
Louise Hobbs	Lilly Myers	21 Sep 1921
Robert Hughs	Marie Baker	21 Sep 1921
Eugene Moore	Sadie Walker	23 Sep 1921
Arlie Hogan	Myrtle Little	23 Sep 1921
Clarence Shelton	May Phillips	24 Sep 1921
Paul D. Wilson	Azzie Lee Aspray	24 Sep 1921
William T. Smith	Lavada Tollison	25 Sep 1921
Odie Edwards	Lena Williams	26 Sep 1921
A. L. Campbell	Ellee Williams	26 Sep 1921
Hugh Nichols	Stella Meadows	30 Sep 1921
Riley Vantrese	Ina Blalock	5 Oct 1921
Alega Yarbro	Mell Upton	5 Oct 1921
Ab Smith	Flora B. Wayne	9 Oct 1921
H. R. Proffer	Maude Skelton	9 Oct 1921
William A. Hemphill Jr.	Ernestine Adair Baldwin	11 Oct 1921

GROOM	BRIDE	SOLEMNIZED
Arthur M. Crim	Lucille Herrell	10 Oct 1921
James I. Edwards	Roxa Williams	16 Oct 1921
Clyde O. Burcham	Cecil Tippett	16 Oct 1921
Eliza Wakefield	Iva Dye	16 Oct 1921
Rayburn Pelts	Ella Baker	14 Oct 1921
William Hedgecock	Corda Sturgeon	14 Oct 1921
Drew Curtis	Cleo Sides	15 Oct 1921
Robert Hall	Kathleen Robertson	15 Oct 1921
Wilburn D. Davis	Cora A. Powell	15 Oct 1921
James Murdough	Grace Fiddler	15 Oct 1921
R. L. Long	Bertha Collins	17 Oct 1921
Arthur Dye	Thelma Troutt	15 Oct 1921
Buell Parks	Erna Cates	15 Oct 1921
Cecil Miller	Effie Hampton	15 Oct 1921
G. W. Jackson	Fannie M. Williams	15 Oct 1921
J. L. Groomes	Mrs. Pheby Shafford	16 Oct 1921
T. J. Nipper	Flossie Cannon	17 Oct 1921
Henry F. Crawford	Lucille Fowler	19 Oct 1921
Otton Leirer	Sybil Burks (Bucks)	30 Oct 1921
George W. Dement	Grace Davidson	23 Oct 1921
Luther Johnson	Etta Hampton	22 Oct 1921
John Wheeling	Mrs. Ida Maines	23 Oct 1921
C. E. Earl	Beulah Brewer	22 Oct 1921
C. Johnson	Hettie Mitchell	24 Oct 1921
Chas. Johnson	Stella Goff	27 Oct 1921
Clarence Ross	Marcel Brydon	26 Oct 1921
Gussie Shands	Dona Stephens	26 Oct 1921
Edie Cades	Sadie Jane Williams	26 Oct 1921
Willie Crafton	Maggie Hamilton	27 Oct 1921
J. F. Lincoln	Liza Revelle	27 Oct 1921
Lowell C. Waltrip	Anna Mae Haislip	30 Oct 1921
M. L. Williams	Mrs. Addie Huggins	29 Oct 1921
W. J. Hutton	Jewell Wright	1 Oct 1921
Joe McMillion	Gladys Terry	1 Oct 1921
James T. Halley	Ollie Pullins	1 Oct 1921
T. O. Stanfill	Mrs. Mary Hale	19 Dec 1921
Elmer Rouse	Mildred Clark	17 Dec 1921
D. P. Gothard	Mrs. Josie Lasswell	17 Dec 1921
Henry N. Hanners	Vina May Odum	19 Dec 1921
Homer Lasswell	Della Cook	17 Dec 1921
John Virgil Waltrip	Bessie Larey	17 Dec 1921
Oscar Springer (col)	Emma Bell (col)	18 Dec 1921
John Brimager	Lela Davidson	19 Dec 1921
W. R. Kinchrow	Emmie Wilkerson	15 Dec 1921

GROOM	BRIDE	SOLEMNIZED
Anderson Black	Lura Dowler	14 Dec 1921
Sunny T. Morris (col)	Ruth Mack (col)	12 Dec 1921
Earl Edwards	Mrs. Ethel Merritt	10 Dec 1921
Olen Snider	Adell Vincent	9 Dec 1921
W. D. Hays	Mrs. Nora Perkins	6 Dec 1921
Fred Elder	Rosa Lamunion	7 Dec 1921
Allan Morrison	Lilly Williams	8 Oct 1921
Everett Hawkins	Myrtle Trije (Tripe)	27 Nov 1921
Johnnie Derry	Zelmar Dickson	28 Dec 1921
Loyd Boss	Florence Harkey	27 Dec 1921
Claud Wagester	Daisy Crafton	27 Dec 1921
Al Bost	Lydia Guien	24 Dec 1921
Oscar Gamble	Rachel Jones	24 Dec 1921
Richard C. Jennings	Lillian Argo	25 Dec 1921
L. C. Tharp	Gladys McAuley	23 Dec 1921
Artie Stoker	May Emma Cox	22 Dec 1921
Earl Waddell	Florence Glover	24 Dec 1921
Baxter Williams	Lora Green (Greer)	21 Dec 1921
Robert Harris	Fernia Ridgeway	21 Dec 1921
Everett Brantlow	Anna Freeman	21 Dec 1921
Homer Crawford	Mrs. Gracie Ricks	4 Jan 1922
J. T. Tilson	Mrs. Florence Johnson	7 Jan 1922
William B. Miller	Lucile Bagby	15 Jan 1922
M. N. Howard	Mrs. Minnie Farley	2 Jan 1922
John Cagle	Mrs. Silvey Frye	13 Jan 1922
W. T. Hicks	Gladys Bennett	14 Jan 1922
Chas. M. Lemasters	Ida M. Shields	16 Jan 1922
Amzie Hampton (col)	Lulu White (col)	13 Jan 1922
Jesse Pate	Hallie Williams	7 Jan 1922
James Harper	Mrs. Margaret Kelley	7 Jan 1922
Commie Ford	Elva Grogan	15 Jan 1922
Benford Bost	Lillie Gentry	15 Jan 1922
J. W. Potillo	Ida M. Ballard	11 Jan 1922
Robert Freeman	Laura May Parish	11 Jan 1922
Nute Gulley	Martie Goff	26 Jan 1922
John R. Nickens	Emma Doggett	8 Jan 1922
John F. McAnally	Pearl Branum	8 Jan 1922
J. P. Longgrear	Christine Guillory	25 Jan 1922
Gromie Bufford (col)	Beatrice Hart (col)	7 Jan 1922
Aussie Pruett	Ruth Baugas (Bangas)	27 Jan 1922
Irla Hunter	Hattie Shafer	22 Jan 1922
Willie Walker	Maudie Hearn	22 Jan 1922
Roy Gooch	Aileen Killion	11 Jan 1922
John McCarty	Katie Rainwater	20 Jan 1922

GROOM	BRIDE	SOLEMNIZED
Dewey Preslar	Edith Mason	2 Jan 1922
Alvin Hampton	Lulu Vincent	4 Jan 1922
Carl Snider	Golda Varner	18 Dec 1922
Sidney F. Grugett	Laurenia Martin	31 Dec 1921
George Johnson	Nell Willmore	31 Dec 1922
Ben H. Rosse	Eva May Rolens	15 Dec 1922
William H. Gwaltney	Eva Petty	24 Dec 1922
Carter Barnes	Ettie Pulley	25 Dec 1921
Thomas G. Spencer	Matilda H. Yohl	4 Jan 1922
James Snider	Pearl Jackson	3 Dec 1921
James W. Stephens	Christine Mitchell	27 Jan 1922
Chris Hager	Della Payne	30 Jan 1922
Arthur Hopkins	Ethel Edmundson	23 Feb 1922
Fredd Peerman	Mrs. Maude B. Milburn	4 Mar 1922
Dave Childers	Mrs. Lela Higlen	12 Feb 1922
Beauford Green	Mrs. Irie Davis	17 Feb 1922
Ott Cravens	Lillian Keys	12 Feb 1922
Albert Cook	Pearl Anderson	15 Feb 1922
Homer Pruett	Lexia Gentry	12 Feb 1922
A. W. Miles	Mrs. Alma Lunsford	16 Feb 1922
Ruben Davenport	Sadie Pruett	10 Feb 1922
Arthur G. Brown	Mrs. Nettie Perry	5 Feb 1922
Percy M. Jones (col)	Leona Jones (col)	21 Feb 1922
Ellis Burks	Jessie Marle Johnson	5 Feb 1922
Roscoe M. Bess	Vera Anderson	5 Feb 1922
Chester Alvey	Josie Ray	6 Feb 1922
J___ Edwards	Mrs. Martha Allen	9 Feb 1922
Ora Metcalf	Marguarite Eddington	10 Feb 1922
Abe Campbell	Bertha Moore	13 Feb 1922
G. H. Cruse	M. M. White	8 Feb 1922
Sidney Wilbanks	Myrtle Graves	13 Feb 1922
Henry A. Morris	Inex Lee Bone	12 Feb 1922
W. H. Blanchard	Rea Mabley	15 Feb 1922
William L. Jackson	Mrs. Minnie Jordan	18 Feb 1922
Edgar Conner	Mrs. Pat Ross	20 Feb 1922
Arvel Pirtle	Blanche Tanner	18 Feb 1922
J. W. Williams	Mrs. Kate Hudson	24 Feb 1922
Elgie Hammond	Willie May Stegall	24 Feb 1922
Ogle Vaughn	Hattie Bost	25 Feb 1922
Clark Warren	Mrs. Nellie Harris	26 Feb 1922
H. H. Moore	Lora Brown	1 Mar 1922
Claud Warren	May Buchanan	26 Feb 1922
J. D. Hays (Harp)	Mrs. Halmae June Hackett	1 Mar 1922
W. M. Crocker	Mrs. Minnie Farris	4 Mar 1922

GROOM	BRIDE	SOLEMNIZED
Revel Maynard	Eula Blackmore	5 Mar 1922
Ochel Davidson	Hellen Roughtloy	6 Mar 1922
Bud Taylor	Pearl Henry	4 Mar 1922
Earl Lock	Cora Barrin	7 Mar 1922
George A. Sutton	Jessie Swain	11 Mar 1922
Ed Patterson	Girty Hodges	9 Mar 1922
Thomas F. Rafforty	Majorie Hall	10 Mar 1922
Chester L. Martin	Ida Hall	12 Mar 1922
Gilbert G. Turner	Mrs. Cora Jarbo	13 Mar 1922
W. T. Emery	Agnes Thrasher	20 Mar 1922
M. L. Looney	Anna Bell	19 Mar 1922
Troy Johnson	Lillian Burton	20 Mar 1922
Glenn Gossett	Bessie Halford	29 Mar 1922
Walter Robertson	Villia Kirby	21 Mar 1922
Richard Pope	Mrs. Zora E. Smith	21 Mar 1922
Calvin Toler	Helen Malin	31 Mar 1922
Frederick A. Becker	Addie Lee Weather	1 Apr 1922
Jessie W. Phillips	Elsie Childers	10 Apr 1922
J. B. Johnson	Mrs. Nancy Barnes	8 Apr 1922
Henry Baker	Edith Buchanan	8 Apr 1922
Chas. L. Rawhoof	Katherine Bennett	7 Apr 1922
E. M. Gregory	Mrs. Clara Skief	6 Apr 1922
Nathan Bolin	Chattie Dye	3 Apr 1922
Henry Gordon	Katie Richardson	1 Apr 1922
Olan Brown	Ella Dockins	1 Apr 1922
David Wineman	Clara James	7 Apr 1922
F. F. Shular	Mrs. Laura Sutt	<u>28 May 1920</u>
Lee Hearn	Ellen Warner	7 Apr 1922
Walter Burke	Kattie Pruett	11 Apr 1922
Chas. Thaxtion	Virgie Clifford	11 Apr 1922
J.M. McKenzie	Alice Weathers	12 Apr 1922
Carlile Thompson	May Higgins	13 Apr 1922
Fred Herrod	Mrs. Arire Poindexter	16 Apr 1922
Walter Ross	Mildred Lewis	15 Apr 1922
Jim Hopkins	Mrs. Ellen Harmon	20 Apr 1922
James Price	Elizabeth Cagle	15 Apr 1922
Hearschell Philips	Alice Philips	15 Apr 1922
Addison Mathis	Valeria Minton	17 Apr 1922
Lon Wells	Eva Wilburn	19 Apr 1922
Plat McConnaughey	Virgie Thompson	18 Apr 1922
W. A. Shahan	Mrs. Elva Scroggins	20 Apr 1922
H. K. Barnes	Norma Gordon	19 Apr 1922
Garfield Hartley	Nora White	21 Apr 1922
Travis Trainer	Flossie Higgason	22 Apr 1922

GROOM	BRIDE	SOLEMNIZED
G. R. Rich	Minnie Duff	Date Not Shown
W. A. Cross	Helen Crider	25 Apr 1922
William C. Vinson	Lela May Moore	27 Apr 1922
H. C. Lloyd	Ellen Dye	29 Apr 1922
Bob Cook	Ida Duncan	1 May 1922
John Harman	Minnie L. Gentry	2 May 1922
C. A. Whitworth	Bell Merritt	6 May 1922
Clarence Bennett	Flora Buckner	5 May 1922
Van Granham	Ruby Chailland	6 May 1922
Louis Pelts	Ola Crim	6 May 1922
I. L. Keown	Katherene Ward	8 May 1922
Earl Ward	Lorena Asher	9 May 1922
Samuel M. Thompson	Luciel Melton	9 May 1922
T. S. Genter	Mrs. Mary E. Parker	13 May 1922
Chas. Johnson	Veda Williams	14 May 1922
Frank Acorns	Maudie Duggins	17 May 1922
A. Bardmass	Myrtle Dye	15 Dec 1921
Geo. J. Baker	Sunshine Butts	24 May 1922
Verney Rattliff	Esther Hatcher	16 Jan/Jun 1922
L. G. Hubbard	Hattie Ward	20 May 1922
G. A. Kersmel	Fannie Hamlin	11 May 1922
A. R. Trailer	Mildred Shyrock	22 Jan 1922
Elza Hopkins	Cora Bell Prater	29 Apr 1922
Raleigh Dill	Mabel Tanner	20 May 1922
John M. Gardner	Fay Daisy Woodall	24 May 1922
Bill Hutchinson	Bertha Pruett	29 May 1922
Levern Parker	Myrtle Gaston	26 May 1922
Hiram Cook	Icie Kiser	28 May 1922
Fred J. Prater	Myrtle Hartwell	27 May 1922
W. R. Turner	Josephine Hall	29 May 1922
William Vandergriff	Mary M. Conway	1 Jul 1922
Jess Brinkley	Nellie Gray	8 Jun 1922
Edgar Samples	Orna Birchfield	16 Jun 1922
James R. Smith	Clara M. Daffron	1 Jul 1922
William F. Miner	Annie Dickinson	22 Jun 1922
Everett J. Langdon	Frennie E. Sherley	22 Jun 1922
Chas. V. McGuire	Della Mooney	17 Jun 1922
Sam Moore	Ethel Lancaster	6 Jun 1922
A. M. Harrison	Mrs. Samantha Bailey	3 Jun 1922
Roy Holifield	Gwendolyn Sullivan	1 Jun 1922
Claude Jones	May Haycraft	6 Jun 1922
C. J. Herrell	Katie Garrett	6 Jun 1922
Will Chambers	Laura Pettyjohn	1 Jun 1922
Oley Neeley	Lora Ward	6 Jun 1922

GROOM	BRIDE	SOLEMNIZED
David Randolph	Anola Russell	19 Jun 1922
Jake Alberson	Stella Hampton	29 Jun 1922
Earchel Singleton	Ethel Boggs	26 Jun 1922
P. M. Snow	Maude Butler	3 Jun 1922
O. J. Johnson	Ethel Doherty	5 Jul 1922
Harry E. Womack	Nellie Gladys Long	9 Jul 1922
T. J. McFarland	Ada Taylor	1 Jul 1922
Lonnie Harpole	Edith Walls	2 Jul 1922
Emmett Lacy	Lena Banthrall	6 Jul 1922
Jacob Henry Weeks	Lertha May Ladyman	3 Jul 1922
Robert Wohrman	Eula Langdon	4 Jul 1922
William Pritchett	Emma Eskew	8 Jul 1922
T. B. Brannon	Mrs. Iona Hooper	4 Jul 1922
Arthur Harris	Bessie Vandine	24 Jun 1922
J. F. Fields	Mrs. May Grady	21 Jan/Jun 1922
James W. Bennett	Pearl Johnson	20 Jun 1922
R. L. Garner	Alverta Carroll	18 Jun 1922
Alfred Roy Carroll	Nettie Norine Smith	18 Jun 1922
William B. Shrum	Emma Taylor	25 Jun 1922
S. Devers	Emma Brinkley	28 Jun 1922
Floyd Hardy	Bonnie Underwood	27 Jun 1922
Lucious G. Snider	Leona Belt	29 Jun 1922
Miles Ellis Burris	Francie Margaret Johnson	10 Jun 1922
Feley M. Kirchen	Myrtle Atkerson	29 Jun 1922
Eliga L. Mitchell	Thelma Marie London	5 Jul 1922
Van Gargas	Pearl Walpole	10 Jul 1922
James L. Horner	Hattie Cullins	4 Jul 1922
Henry P. Carroll	Jessie Hannah	9 Jul 1922
Albert Brotherton	Ada Whitehead	7 Jul 1922
Peter A. H. Honnell	Edna A. Collins	6 Jul 1922
Elbert Ferrell	Millie Crafford	9 Jul 1922
George Pickering	Ida Hardy	10 Jul 1922
C. L. Mikel	Myrtle Blanton	20 Aug 1922
A. J. Beavers	Mrs. Mary Beavers	13 Sep 1922
Henry Edgar Klein	Maudie Myrtle Smith	12 Sep 1922
G. W. Whitehead	Willie Lee	9 Sep 1922
Harvey Austin	Sybil Austin	9 Mar 1922 (Sept)
T. G. Minter	Mrs. Lilliah McNeely	9 Sep 1922
Dave Johnson	Flora Gatewood	9 Sep 1922
Jessie Wilson	Alice E. Pyles	9 Sep 1922
Charles Morris	Goldie Case	9 Sep 1922
O. N. Bohannon	Lillian Turpin	10 Sep 1922
John B. Pickering	Effie M. McIntosh	6 Sep 1922
William Whitehouse	Velma Newton	2 Sep 1922

GROOM	BRIDE	SOLEMNIZED
E. O. Bridges	Dora Ridings	2 Sep 1922
William C. Darden	Roda Pitts	2 Sep 1922
Z. L. Kerby	Edith Jenkins	3 Sep 1922
Charley Young (col)	Edie Farrar (col)	3 Sep 1922
V. L. Snider	Lucy C. Pennington	2 Sep 1922
Alton Tatom	Gladys Ridge	31 Aug 1922
Earl Mason	Goldie Gaskins	27 Aug 1922
Milton Hicks	Rebecca Pendigrass	26 Aug 1922
E. Wheeler	Martha McDaniel	24 Aug 1922
James W. Cain	Helen Higginbotham	31 Aug 1922
G. T. Heath	Dovie Billops	24 Aug 1922
A. M. Singleton	Mrs. M. T. Edwards	Date Not Shown
John Snider	Dovie Powers	Date Not Shown
W. V. Stacy	Lorene Wright	17 Aug 1922
W. R.Hale	Mrs. Pearl Miller	17 Aug 1922
Fred Esterline	Effie Thomas	16 Aug 1922
Arthur Massey	Gladys Stovall	16 Aug 1922
Troy C. Ennis	Francis E. Baugh	17 Aug 1922
Nelson Austin	Lillie Mofield	15 Aug 1922
Earl R. Eakers	Irene Wright	13 Aug 1922
Charley H. Barnes	Obra T. Davidson	13 Aug 1922
Otto Gross	Bertha Allen	7 Aug 1922
J. L. Robinson	Willie Houston	5 Aug 1922
Homer Lancaster	Pearlie Lee Davis	7 Aug 1922
F. M. Burton	Rosie Willis	5 Aug 1922
W. A. Holbrook	Mrs. Martha Holbrook	5 Aug 1922
Henry Lee Lawrence	Emma Edith Cook	5 Aug 1922
Lexie Lee Taylor	Mamie Throgmorton	6 Aug 1922
Ezery Medley	Kate Halter	5 Aug 1922
Velva Stacy	Bennie Ham	2 Aug 1922
John Willinski	Eleanor Fitzgerald	2 Aug 1922
G. C. Wadley	Suddie Davidson	1 Aug 1922
C. Perkins	Anna Grooms	29 Jul 1922
Albert Scarlet	Bertha Naile	30 Jul 1922
A. H. Perry	Mrs. Mollie Drewry	29 Jul 1922
Willie L. Avery	Dollie Turner	29 Jul 1922
Willie Farrar (col)	Hyresia King (col)	28 Jul 1922
Sherd Johnson	Uvah Barton	27 Jul 1922
A. J. Davenport	M. J. Hart	27 Jul 1922
Joseph Hill	Mrs. Addie Esters	25 Jul 1922
William Byrd	Anna Johnson	26 Jul 1922
R. R. Richardson	Mabel Gorden	24 Jul 1922
James Goodnight	May Jones	24 Jul 1922
Ernest White	Buelah Wells	24 Jul 1922

GROOM	BRIDE	SOLEMNIZED
Selmar Tate	Bessie Edwards	23 Jul 1922
Herbert Showmaker	Irene Tular Stokes	22 Jul 1922
Albert Mangrum	Cassie Watkins	19 Jul 1922
Vernie S. Walker	Rosa Lee Blackburn	22 Jul 1922
J. A. Bridges	Mrs. Anna Hunter	18 Jul 1922
Virgil V. Oatman	F. C. Smith	18 Jul 1922
Bill Layton	Elsy Irene Tuttleton	15 Jul 1922
Aaron Arvel Gibbs	Bertha May Elder	4 Jul 1922
Lenos (Levos) White	Lillie Sissom	21 Jun 1922
Clarence Russel	Mrs. Becca Russel	17 May 1922
O. B. Goodnight	Rena James	13 May 1922
Malcom Clark	Elvin Owens	12 Sep 1922
E. A. Binkley	Elsie Gammons	14 Sep 1922
W. White	Goldie Cobb	14 Sep 1922
Almos England	Pearl Sparks	16 Sep 1922
Robert Dyer	Gladys Hale	16 Sep 1922
C. E. Hale	Loone Oliver	16 Sep 1922
Junous Garrett	Ella Goode	16 Sep 1922
W. F. Frudenberg	Dovie Barnwell	16 Sep 1922
T. D. Wyett	M. S. Blakes	19 Sep 1922
Ara Green Paul	Minnie Karlish	19 Sep 1922
W. D. Veatch	Silvia Williams	19 Sep 1922
L. S. Pry	Bessie Leffel	19 Sep 1922
R. H. Adams	Juanity Tilford	20 Sep 1922
Barney Clifton	Ollie M. Turner	26 Sep 1922
A. E. Waters	Violet _. Fudge	26 Sep 1922
J. A. Morrison	Cora May Chism	25 Sep 1922
James A. Fisher	Myrtle L. McElain	26 Sep 1922
Jesse Hawkins	Essie Johnson	23 Sep 1922
H. B. Stephens	Clara Hall	20 Sep 1922
Jess Wingate	Gertie V. Smith	18 Sep 1922
Loran Newell	Bertha Nunley	16 Sep 1922
John Underwood	Lena Back	16 Sep 1922
Charles O. Williams	May Causey	14 Sep 1922
Simon E. Eberhard	Mary Ubelhoe	27 Sep 1922
Frank Cook	Ada Alisher	30 Sep 1922
Albert Lester	Bera Tippit	28 Sep 1922
Everet Morgan	Lillie May Taylor	23 Sep 1922
Ovle Mason	Opal Hayden	17 Sep 1922
Raymond Engleheart	Opal Huffman	18 Sep 1922
David Powell	Ethel Blanchard	5 Oct 1922
J. I. Cabaness	Cora Tigett (Ligett)	5 Oct 1922
W. Binkley	Mrs. T. M. Richards	4 Oct 1922
Henry Wiyatt	Alice Lindsey	3 Oct 1922

GROOM	BRIDE	SOLEMNIZED
Charlie Jackson	Gladys Shepard	2 Oct 1922
Russel Vaughn	Mrs. Florence Smith	8 Oct 1922
Harvey Kaiser	Lue Ethel Hyatt	1 Oct 1922
F. J. Bowen	Ethyl M. Whitwell	30 Sep 1922
Melvin Birchfield	Helen James	1 Oct 1922
Newton Hunsaker	Anna Dublin	30 Sep 1922
Fred Reid (Reed)	Dollie Boyd	1 Oct 1922
Charles A. Greenfield	Ethel Carroll	30 Sep 1922
Ed Stephens	Flora Tune	14 Oct 1922
Lewis Hamilton	Latha Vaughn	13 Oct 1922
Lloyd Graves	Irene Brimer	12 Oct 1922
Doyle Gaines	Priscilla Maclin	9 Oct 1922
Willie Hallett	Myrtle Ross	7 Oct 1922
James Williams	Dolphie Hampton	8 Oct 1922
Raymond Robertson	Ruby Pointer	7 Oct 1922
Charlie Owens	Lessie Napiere	8 Oct 1922
Jodie Mills	Ida Daily	7 Oct 1922
H. J. Pope	Nell Bratchard	7 Oct 1922
Lee Manley	Esther McDurham	7 Oct 1922
Robert J. Davis	Flo Lewis	6 Oct 1922
E. A. Thomann	Katherene Lemmens	3 Oct 1922
Benard Davenport	Ella Childs	8 Oct 1922
James Brahdon	Agnes Powell	6 Oct 1922
Robert B. Wright	Bulah Pruett	6 Oct 1922
Robert Oakes	Louise Dye	7 Oct 1922
I. R. Bostwick	Ola Maccune	30 May 1922
Ira Coffell	Ocie Wilson	30 Sep 1922
Wilbert Langley	Gretrude Ross	1 Oct 1922
Thomas H. Neely	Rosey Ward	4 Oct 1922
A. L. Alexander	Madge Drake	17 Oct 1922
Lawrence Them	Mamie Dample	27 Oct 1922
Ivory Preyer	Kethereif Bubach	25 Oct 1922
Robert Rodgers	Hettie Fretwell	25 Oct 1922
Dave Willoby	Beulah Lands	21 Oct 1922
Aloys Michel	Lena Stalle	25 Oct 1922
Guss Carmack	Beatrice Roy	14 Oct 1922
Freeman Wagoner	Helen Karlish	31 Oct 1922
Phillip T. Bell	Mrs. Nettie Miller	19 Oct 1922
Jake Fruck	Teresa Myrtle Hoyclen	17 Oct 1922
John McCormick	Bessie Stephens	21 Oct 1922
Willie Herrin	Sadie Fleetwood	15 Oct 1922
Homer Odell	Mayme Muse	16 Oct 1922
Lester McFadden	Edna Bridges	15 Oct 1922
Troy Wineman	Ellin Horsman	15 Oct 1922

GROOM	BRIDE	SOLEMNIZED
Luther Elsworth	Emma Rainey	13 Oct 1922
Arvel Earl	Mamie Scott	14 Oct 1922
Frank Holland	Nora Mathis	17 Oct 1922
Oscar Hartwell	Josie McRill	18 Oct 1922
Chas. Stephens	Lessie Foster	20 Oct 1922
Winford Ramsey	Bessie Sorrel	21 Oct 1922
Lige Etheridge	Ruby Avery	30 Oct 1922
Floyd York	Opal Berry	3 Oct 1922
Cecil Latham	Nealy Baker	30 Oct 1922
Ouil O'neal	Lenora Veaniule	28 Oct 1922
Jesse Simms	Myrtle Brooks	31 Oct 1922
Henery Jackson	Gertrude Earley	28 Oct 1922
Arch Brown	Jewell Thompson	31 Oct 1922
Rube Moore	Emma Easley	4 Nov 1922
R. S. Jeffers	Grace Duncan	1 Nov 1922
August Perkins	Ethey Young	11 Nov 1922
W. E. Watson	Willie Oliver	18 Nov 1922
Thos. Young	Ruth Kenser	15 Nov 1922
Geo. Price	Bonnie Holcomb	16 Nov 1922
John Hackworth	Flora Smith	14 Nov 1922
James Greenfield	Dollie Coleman	15 Nov 1922
W. P. Edmonston	Molly Rhodes	11 Nov 1922
Wayne Sisk	Viola Martin	11 Nov 1922
Earnest Smotherman	Hulda George	10 Jun 1922
Louis Loyd	Rosa Abraham	12 Nov 1922
Ira Doherty	Lena Gateley	11 Nov 1922
W. M. Huffman	Edith Wells	13 Nov 1922
Eugene Queen	Cora Derryberry	5 Nov 1922
William A. Pruett	Sadie Brown	9 Nov 1922
Clyde Deck	Bertie Ray	9 Nov 1922
Albert Cunningham	Lucille Howard	12 Nov 1922
M. L. Bodine	Millie Blain	12 Nov 1922
Sonnie Downing	Virginia Harwood	8 Nov 1922
Bertha Clark	Margaret Elderbrook	11 Nov 1922
Wayne Staples	Pearl Deycus	8 Nov 1922
Coy Banister	Mae Smith	6 Nov 1922
Fred V. Barns	Ruth Aldridge	4 Nov 1922
Chas. Miles	Ida Adams	5 Nov 1922
Arthur Foster	Zelma Donica	4 Nov 1922
Geo. Cox	Lottie Silkey	5 Nov 1922
Orbe Grouch	Emma Gouldman	5 Nov 1922
Jesse Arnold	Sudie Glass	9 Dec 1922
Charlie Baugher	Marie Followell	30 Dec 1922
D. B. Blackburn	Lula Wells	2 Dec 1922

GROOM	BRIDE	SOLEMNIZED
Everett Berry	Pearl Palmer	11 Dec 1922
Willie R. Bazzell	Bessie Cagle	24 Nov 1922
W. Baker	C. E. Miles	9 Dec 1922
Chas. Bowden	Loula Thomas	1 Nov 1922
Walter Bosse	Ruth Shultz	12 Dec 1922
George Brown	Delcie Oneil	24 Dec 1922
Albert Bushong	Orah Ragsdale	11 Dec 1922
John V. Burgess	Sarah Moddle	22 Dec 1922
Ben. H. Cannon	Mary Tierce	27 Nov 1922
Clarence Clark	Lillian Dye	21 Dec 1922
Arthur Clark	Pansey Shelby	20 Dec 1922
John D. Davis	Luella Brown	24 Dec 1922
James W. Doherty	Mildred G. Abernathy	2 Dec 1922
Claude Donoho	Elizabeth Vanflaugh	21 Nov 1922
Courtland Dyer	Elsie Clinton	24 Dec 1922
Thomas J. Estes	Mary D. Faulkner	23 Dec 1922
Elmer Eubanks	Hester Fry	23 Dec 1922
William Curtis Eaton	Emma Gothard	5 Dec 1922
William R. Evans	Mrs. Jennie Bailey	11 Dec 1922
Ed Frazier	Ruth Olliver	3 Dec 1922
Leonard Followell	Druzella Adams	14 Dec 1922
Earnest Green	Dicie Vincent	24 Dec 1922
L. B. Guthrie	Mary Bailey	24 Nov 1922
Richard Gilpin	Bertha Coleman	25 Nov 1922
Virgil Garrett	Ruth B. Austill	19 Dec 1922
Vernon Golightly	Elsie Darenell	25 Nov 1922
Thomas Gerry	Mary Kean	28 Nov 1922
Charlie Going	Syble Smith	29 Nov 1922
Austin Gabriel	Manda Johnson	6 Dec 1922
Carl Green	Blanche Shores	29 Oct 1922
Clint Haney	Mrs. Rose Roberts	20 Dec 1922
Bill Harrison	Grace Mangale	2 Dec 1922
W. T. Ingram	Mrs. Nettie Shands	23 Nov 1922
Loyd Jewell	Loise L. Higan	29 Nov 1922
Logan Jackson	Orba Farmer	6 Dec 1922
Harry Jones	Mary Jennings	20 Dec 1922
B. F. Kimbrel	Agnes Gamblin	25 Nov 1922
William G. Kendall	Anna Nalezinck	9 Dec 1922
Roy Koons	Lottie Ponder	25 Nov 1922
Schley Lee	Lula Huffman	25 Nov 1922
Henry Lands	Lillie Harris	10 Nov 1922
Clyde Myers	Esther Keith	18 Nov 1922
Clinton Mitchell	Leota Lance	26 Nov 1922
Cecil Morris	Lizzie Dubar	16 Dec 1922

GROOM	BRIDE	SOLEMNIZED
Arthur Moore	Goldie Dartt	29 Nov 1922
Rube Moore	Bobbie Cagle	9 Dec 1922
Douglass Montgomery	Eppie Ray	8 Dec 1922
Ethel McClain	Lillie Blanton	27 Nov 1922
Melvin G. McElwrath	Nellie Nixon	23 Dec 1922
Vernell Obbards	Eunice Williams	20 Dec 1922
James L. O'Neal	Casey Lee Ogle	24 Dec 1922
William Pendleton Earls	Sallie Montgomery	24 Nov 1922
Ed Pruett	Clara Cashion	18 Nov 1922
Numie Provow	Martha L. Roberds	2 Dec 1922
W. T. Ray	Lena Henslee	24 Dec 1922
H. E. Rule	Jessie Kennedy	16 Dec 1922
Auto R. Riney	Laura Luckett	2 Dec 1922
R. L. Robinson	Ola Ollford	2 Dec 1922
Cletus M. Smith	Vivian Barney	26 Dec 1922
Clyde Sanders	Dora Ellen Burden	30 Dec 1922
Henry Smith	Lena Harper	25 Nov 1922
Thomas Sullinger	Lottie Pherson	25 Nov 1922
John Sinden	Paulene Roland	21 Nov 1922
Levi Sneed	Beulah Carry	18 Dec 1922
Dillard Slankard	Lora Snider	20 Dec 1922
W. A. Stacks	Martha Edwards	23 Dec 1922
Virgil Trainer	Sarah House	24 Dec 1922
Roy Lee Turner	Lena Robertson	6 Dec 1922
Homer Vincent	Pansy Brown	14 Oct 1922
Ivan Venable	Celia McAuliff	9 Dec 1922
William Welch	Elsie Sprague	25 Nov 1922
J. M. Waltrip	Birdie Horton	23 Nov 1922
Gorden Wright	Myrtie Craig	1 Dec 1922
Alvin Workman	Viola Clark	5 Dec 1922
Robert Lee Williams	Katy Herrell	9 Dec 1922
Clarence Young	Nettie Biggs	19 Dec 1922
W. M. Aldous	Lydia Francis Chatam	31 Dec 1922
W. T. Bledsoe	Flossie Matthews	9 Jan 1923
Sam Common	Anna Howard	10 Jan 1923
Clois Lee Gales	Myrtle Kendrex	6 Jan 1923
Glover Jaques	Myrtle Welker	6 Jan 1923
Alonzo Jackson Keating	Margarette Cobb	28 Dec 1922
Daniel Masterson	Myrtle M. Looney	2 Jan 1923
Lar__ce Mobley	Irene Durham	2 Jan 1923
Gilbert Moore	Francis Cobb	6 Jan 1923
Shelton Pelts	Marie Sullivan	31 Dec 1923
Willie Petty	Sylvia Long	3 Jan 1923
W. Proffer	Alma Grissom	1 Jan 1923

GROOM	BRIDE	SOLEMNIZED
Henry Rideout	Myrtle Smith	8 Jan 1923
Syble D. Ramsey	Rosie Mae Summerfield	1 Jan 1923
Claud Sullinger	Allie Holt	6 Jan 1923
Gilbert Smith	Jessie Woods	29 Dec 1922
Ernest Smith	Mrs. Allie Mitchell	2 Jan 1923
Jimmie Thomas	Marie Madding	18 Dec 1922
A. B. Thomas	Mrs. Ellen Edwards	4 Jan 1923
B. H. Wicker	Mavis Skaggs	1 Jan 1923
E. L. Yearry	Flora Kuhn	1 Jan 1923
W. L. Adams	Lessie May Cunningham	13 Jan 1923
Ray Moxley	Sidney M. Shultz	12 Jan 1923
William Whitacre	Irene Brett	14 Jan 1923
J. W. Brodie	Mrs. Dennie Hood	13 Jan 1923
Stanley McCurter	Alma Qualls	13 Jan 1923
D. J. Samples	Minnie Williams	13 Jan 1923
W. F. Smallwood	Mrs. Mary Elizabeth Lindsey	16 Jan 1923
Claud Witt	Dixie Perkins	29 Jan 1923
L. E. Baugher	Annie Smith	27 Jan 1923
L. C. Martin	Edith Faust	28 Jan 1923
C. H. Herrin	Adah Taylor	28 Jan 1923
Frank Brewer	Maggie Pool	28 Jan 1923
Thomas Davis	Brooksy Miller	27 Jan 1923
M. T. Blaine	Hester Davis	20 Jan 1923
Otis Small	Susie Sanders	24 Jan 1923
Clarence Summers	Florence Allen	20 Jan 1923
Claud Aldridge	Mrs. Bessie Aldridge	24 Jan 1923
Jess Ratcliff	Milicent Dunn	24 Jan 1923
S. R. Longgrear	Tera Walker	26 Nov 1923 (1922)
T. C. Caldwell	Mrs. Ruby Smith	16 Jan 1923
Herbert Ray	Myrtle Pruett	19 Dec 1922
Floyd Ladyman	Betty Damron	19 Dec 1922
Clarence Hillary Smiley	Mrs. Eva Comal Darnell	30 Jan 1923
Bon Carter	Josie Miller	31 Jan 1923
A. T. Harris	Melissa Ridgeway	14 Jan 1923
Ben Tucker	Gracie Burkit	31 Jan 1923
Gene Deck	Nora Poe	29 Jan 1923
Elmer Edwards	Flossie Taylor	13 Jan 1923
Herman Carter	Nellie Crawford	23 Jan 1923
Margin Julian	Effie Robertson	21 Jan 1923
Henry Cook	Emma Lane	20 Jan 1923
Walter Ault	Fannie Meharg	16 (nothing else)
J. M. Waldrop	Lucy Willis	19 Jan 1923
Clint Busby	Orna Snider	2 Feb 1923
Dr. J. J. Drace	Gladys Arthur	4 Feb 1923

GROOM	BRIDE	SOLEMNIZED
D. D. Evans	Loucile Duke	3 Feb 1923
Samuel S. Frederick	Mrs. Mary J. Lamasters	6 Feb 1923
Charlie Keck	Sabie Cole	5 Feb 1923
W. R. Myers	Gusta Harvell	4 Feb 1923
E. R. Patee	May Stegall	5 Feb 1923
Estele Rogers	Bertha Greer	31 Jan 1923
Guy Spillers	Ruby White	30 Jan 1923
Perry White	Gurtie Brewer	3 Feb 1923
Westley Taylor	Edna Frazer	26 Jan 1923
J. P. Martin	Hattie Wallace	2 Mar 1923
C. E. James	Pearl Mable Cobb	1 Mar 1923
Thurman Holcomb	Flossie Walkins	1 Mar 1923
Virgil Palston (Polston)	Mrs. Beattress Ferguson	25 Feb 1923
T. F. Hargraves	Effie G. Ward	3 Mar 1923
Troy Rice	Ruth Layton	3 Mar 1923
H. L. Sellers	Grace Gootley	11 Feb 1923
George Jackson	Pearl Spence	12 Feb 1923
Lloyd Good	Pearl Bledsoe	12 Feb 1923
Charles Arnold	Harriet Lewis	16 Feb 1923
M. V. Ayres	Emma Brown	16 Feb 1923
Elmer Collins	Winnie Zechery	22 Jan 1923
Carl Looney	Elizabeth Jones	13 Feb 1923
Charles Back	Ethel Hartle	14 Feb 1923
Clarence O. Edwards	Ellen Biggs	15 Feb 1923
Charles F. Barnes	Icy L. Smyth	22 Mar 1923
J. M. Clark	Mary J. Sikes	18 Mar 1923
Bennie French	Ethel Swinney	18 Mar 1923
Herman Blazier	Mrs. Vider Dunum	17 Mar 1923
Carl Ragsdale	Ella Davis	18 Mar 1923
Albert Stultz	Mable Samples	16 Mar 1923
Ralph Ham	Grace Thomas	15 Feb 1923
Charley Grimes	Delphia Smith	16 Feb 1923
Walter Finch	Bessie Rose	19 Feb 1923
Guiford Johnson	Ella Abernathy	18 Feb 1923
Lee Riddle	Rody Potts	19 Feb 1923
Earl Surber	Ida Puckett	23 Feb 1923
Lee Hughs	Bissie Hanks	21 Feb 1923
W. N. Orr	Mildred Black	3 Mar 1923
Carl North	Edith Harrison	4 Mar 1923
Loyal Cooper	Lelah Coquella Gwaltney	3 Mar 1923
Everett Hayden	Fern Cisco	13 Feb 1923
Elmer McElyea	Flora Frederick	3 Mar 1923
Clifford Pate	Minnie Nolen	6 Mar 1923
Edgar Varnier	Mary E. Coffee	3 Mar 1923

GROOM	BRIDE	SOLEMNIZED
Louis Taylor	Ellen Stanley	12 Mar 1923
Benny N. Hanera	Eva May Homes	254 Feb 1923
R. B. Seal	Mrs. D. Peeden	8 Mar 1923
E. W. Harris	Pearl M. Wyrick	9 Mar 1923
B. L. Walker	Alma Cavoy	6 Mar 1923
John Emmette Alvey	Liddie Fulkerson	3 Mar 1923
I. F. Welty	Beulah Batchelor	11 Mar 1923
Ethridge Phillips	Ora Price	13 Mar 1923
Harry W. Brockman	Bertha Snider	14 Feb 1923
John McDowell	Gladys Vinyard	7 Mar 1923
William Ernest Edmondson	Laura May Davis	9 Feb 1923
Verdo Anderson	Lessie Hannah	11 Feb 1923
Robert Harver	Dessie Byram	25 Jan 1923
John B. Patterson	Mattie Drake	24 Feb 1923
Claude Basham	Pearl Collins	27 Feb 1923
S. C. Scott	Vina Ladyman	26 Feb 1923
Dave Rittenberry	Vinia Belt	25 Feb 1923
G. W. Thompson	Pearl Bess	26 Feb 1923
Fines Winford	Ruth Young	26 Feb 1923
Sam Starr	Mamie Hopkins	24 Feb 1923
S. H. Martin	Floy Wood	17 Feb 1923
Von Chapman	Gazle Ragsdale	7 Feb 1923
Ray Pendleton	Sennella McDermott	11 Feb 1923
T. C. Ham	Etta Katheryn Rose	30 Jan 1923
Clarence Markle	Sadie Pearman	28 Jan 1923
Roy Wittenberry	Maudie Carter	23 Feb 1923
Joe Bracy	Ida Thornton	10 Mar 1923
L. R. McComb	Josie E. Fowler	28 Mar 1923
George Trout	Daisey Bryant	26 Mar 1923
W. C. Chilton	Mrs. Minnie Pendergrass	22 Mar 1923
Carl B. Blair	Mrs. Nelle Brown Bungler	23 Mar 1923
Floyd C. Morrison	Glady L. Goodin	3 Mar 1923
Wayne Pearce	Beulah Bone	30 Mar 1923
Earl Johnson	Aleene Derryberry	2 Apr 1923
H. S. Skidmore	Grace Back	3 Apr 1923
Bill Wilson	Beatrice Frailey	4 Apr 1923
Ben Clanin	Lottie Mansker (Mausker)	7 Apr 1923
Everet Anderson	Rosie Phillips	5 Apr 1923
Tom McMahon	Blanche Nichols	24 Mar 1923
Tom Starr	Gertrude Luke	7 Apr 1923
George Morton	Mrs. Camlee Lemmond	3 Apr 1923
C. B. Houston	Vallie Bird	5 Apr 1923
Jim Gardner	Rosie Barron	24 Mar 1923
John Workman	Lucy Harver (Harner)	8 Apr 1923

GROOM	BRIDE	SOLEMNIZED
Gus A. Johnson	Maudie Franklin	10 Apr 1923
Wayne Huffines	Ethel Haire	11 Apr 1923
Henry Trout	Grace B. Swanner	18 Apr 1923
Horma Phelps	Bernadean Braud	31 Mar 1923
Elmer Burchett	Esther Lale	31 Mar 1923
A. W. Cox	Fannie I. Yount	1 Apr 1923
Walter Hays	Pearl S. Thompson	15 Apr 1923
W. T. Couch	Mrs. Sarah Mabe	16 Apr 1923
James O. Warwick	Cora Kills	18 Apr 1923
Willis Pitman	Lottie Anderson	2 Jun 1923
Thomas Bosley	Hazel B. Thomas	1 Jun 1923
James Smith	Mamie Roark	18 Apr 1923
Moody Horn	Ora May Shipman	17 Apr 1923
Christian Keeper	Mary Catherine Vanderfeltz	26 Apr 1923
Perdie Walls	Myrtle England	22 Apr 1923
V. H. Woodmansee	Marie Gardner	18 Apr 1923
J. E. Sale	Lorine Cox	21 Apr 1923
Earl Harris	Lela Davenport	19 Apr 1923
Cecil Winberry	Nina Gibson	18 Apr 1923
J. W. Vinyard	Belle Lowery	16 Jan 1923
Claude Lebo	Mildred Martin	27 Jun 1923
Curtis Wicks	Ruby Agnes Petijohn	22 Jun 1923
Grady Wofford	Gladys Hodges	23 Jun 1923
W. J. Eulett	E. L. Hodge	25 Jun 1923
John Halder	Jessie Bailey	24 Jun 1923
C. N. Nester	Dellar Crow	23 Jun 1923
Carl B. Crackel	Mary M. Miller	16 Jun 1923
W. T. Brurey	Laura Fisackerly	17 Jan 1923
G. B. Ezell	Carrie May McSwain	9 Jan 1923
John W. Hampton	Mary Alma Muerer	Date Not Shown
C. T. Howard	Bertha Cunningham	3 Jun 1923
Harvey Collins	Rebecca Taylor	16 Jun 19223
E. E. Johnson	Nora Armstrong	15 Jun 1923
J. B. Holloway	Grace Coffel	5 May 1923
Cleo Taylor	Lessie Bowers	9 Jun 1923
Manuel Sturgis	Marie Ballard	18 May 1923
Earl Burk	Mrs. Sadie Pump	30 Apr 1923
T. F. Hopkins	Fannie Dolth	15 May 1923
Lester Statler	Rebecca Williams	13 May 1923
C. M. Lemons	Edna Lewis	19 May 1923
W. J. Allen	Mrs. Edna Hodges	14 May 1923
Carral Presley	Sadie Lentz	26 May 1923
Jessie G. Joncs	Mrs. Dollie Shields	12 May 1923
P. A. McDougal	Pansey Johnson	13 May 1923

GROOM	BRIDE	SOLEMNIZED
C. W. Woods	Mrs. Eveline Tuttle	11 May 1923
W. A. Hawkins	May Dickey	14 May 1923
J. W. Owens	Janie Fisk	10 May 1923
Wayne Dockins	Bessie Hope	12 May 1923
William H. Thompson	Viola Hart	9 May 1923
A. B. Gaddis	Vergie Thorne	9 May 1923
Amos Dowdy	Melva Middleton	6 Jun 1923
Charlie Faulkner	Willie Robertson	9 Jul 1923
Albert Robertson	Annie Reel	8 Jul 1923
Wiley Kendrix	Marie Riggins	9 May 1923
Sam Thornton	Nellie Collins	7 May 1923
Tommy Jones	Clara Edmonds	6 May 1923
H. R. Smith	Malinda Scott	30 Jun 1923
Landis Taylor	Lula Shrout	14 Apr 1923
William L. Smith	Lucinda Fowler	5 May 1923
G. W. McKinzie	Pearl Hutchinson	5 May 1923
Willie Anderson	Dessie Pittman	21 Apr 1923
Ed Little	Maud Deck	2 May 1923
Willie McClish	Ollie Varney	4 May 1923
W. A. Shields	Kate Horner (Harver)	14 Apr 1923
Gaspert Krapf	Anna Philpmine Siebert	2 May 1923
J. F. Craft (Croft)	Iva F. Masters	2 May 1923
James F. Thompson	Norma Lasswell	18 May 1923
Robert Cobb	Ada Hodge	20 May 1923
George Masterson	Nettie Brown	21 Apr 1923
Herbert Miller	Iva Yeley	21 Apr 1923
J. U. Yarbro	Mattie Meeks	21 Apr 1923
Lyman Crites	Mable Lang	22 Apr 1923
Fred Smith	Edna Dillingham	31 Mar 1923
W. G. Neal	Lillie Romines	23 Apr 1923
Manford Slaughter	Mrs. Dessie Alvey	28 Apr 1923
J. W. Singleton	Frona Woods	1 May 1923
Otis Dover	Mrytle Cassey	29 Apr 1923
Will Johnson	Carrie McBride	29 Apr 1923
Sam Pendleton	Cary Britt	23 Jul 1923
Cecil Carnal	Opal Heflin	Date Not Shown
B. F. Sanders	Liva May Blevins	12 Jul 1923
Leonard T. Spencer	Arsuela Phillips	4 Jul 1923
Leslie Husband	Velma Ne__	15 Jul 1923
W. R. Ford	Jewell Lovlace	15 Jul 1923
Claud Venable	Thelma Koonce	15 Jul 1923
J. T. Palmer	Mrs. Annie P. Perry	18 Jun 1923
Charley Damron	Dorothy Bales	10 Jul 1923
H. D. Parker	Murrell Lewis	30 Jun 1923

GROOM	BRIDE	SOLEMNIZED
Elmer Harkey	Mrs. Annie Vardell	14 Jul 1923
W. Elder	Mildred Compton	15 Jul 1923
Nathan Cato	Mrs. Verdie Vaught	16 Jul 1923
Herbert Crider	Edna Wheeler	22 Jul 1923
Willie Lenard	Opal Redmon	7 Jul 1923
Roy Leonburger	Minnie Thompson	21 Jul 1923
Wilburn McIntosh	Bertha Harris	5 Jul 1923
Oscar Redfairn	Erma Huntsing	25 Jul 1923
John Ford	Mrs. Janie Stanley	27 Jul 1923
Robert Shaw	Mrs. Bertha Smith	25 Jul 1923
Robert W. Taylor	Mrs. Attie A. Stackhouse	25 Jul 1923
Luther Laden	Mrs. Ollie Pettijohn	30 Apr 1923
W. J. Dunklin	Louise Pollock	26 Jul 1923
Sam Johnson (col)	Mrs. Fannie Thomas (col)	25 Jul 1923
J. I. Kennedy	Mary Mable Whitehead	28 Jul 1923
Bert Greenway	Ruby Chambers	29 Jul 1923
Ora Johnson	Athel Davis	31 Jul 1923
Walter Runyon	Lemma Bee McIlvoy	28 Jul 1923
Gailon Mallory	Gracie McDermott	3 Aug 1923
Andrew A. Angstrom	Theresa Weidenbenner	1 Aug 1923
D. A. McAnally	Lora Young	4 Aug 1923
C. L. Simmons	Mrs. Lillie Shaffer	4 Aug 1923
Howard L. Vinson	Iris Davidinson	4 Aug 1923
A. F. Mayo	Violet Cagle	6 Aug 1923
Ben Stone	Mrs. Violet Waldrip	7 Aug 19223
Robert Moore (col)	Edna Anderson (col)	6 Aug 1923
Clyde Lemonds	Mary Nixon	7 Aug 1923
Fred H. Hampton	Golda May Smothers	4 Aug 1923
Laren Riggs	Otra Turnbow	8 Aug 1923
Henry DeLong	Helen Philpot	9 Aug 1923
J. M. Williamson	Martha Puckett	11 Aug 1923
Chester E. Walker	Viola Spencer	11 Aug 1923
Charles E. Roper	Elizabeth V. Westerfield	11 Aug 1923
Tom Fleeman	Julia Rose	12 Aug 1923
Ed Davis	Rosa Taylor	3 Jul 1923
Conrad Thompson	Brodie Williams	18 Aug 1923
L. B. Thompson	Sadie Rose	18 Aug 1923
William Samples	Mrs. Renda C. James	18 Aug 1923
Joe Howard	Lona Gore	18 Aug 1923
Marvin Vandiver	Lillie Midkiff	18 Aug 1923
Wallace Gilliam	Dixie Cates	18 Aug 1923
Freeman Bray	Clella Hargraves	16 Aug 1923
Earl McFarland	Clara Templeton	14 Aug 1923
Louie Young	Blanche Thacker	13 Aug 1923

GROOM	BRIDE	SOLEMNIZED
Arthur Colwell	Mrs. Dicie Bibbs	16 Aug 1923
Jessie W. Burks	Mrs. Myrtle Moore	16 Aug 1923
D. Cruce	Mattie Fleetwood	20 Aug 1923
Alex Sternberg	Mrs. Laura Plunkett	21 Aug 1923
Glen Metheny	Della Hyde	22 Aug 1923
Cecil Kinney	Liddie Denbow	22 Aug 1923
Leslie M. Belt	Fleetie Vandiver	21 Jul 1923
James Coleman	Mrs. Ida Boyd	24 Aug 1923
W. P. King	Edna Stone	26 Aug 1923
Arch Limbaugh	Mary Killian	18 Aug 1923
W. McWilliams	Mrs. Mary Cooper	25 Aug 1923
William A. Smithwick	Lennnie Low	29 Aug 1923
W. H. Windle	Mrs. Emma Emery	25 Aug 1923
Chas. Thomas McLeskey	Bertie Coffel	27 Aug 1923
G. W. Householder	Mary Duffy	1 Sep 1923
Charley Bost	Ida Blanch Davis	2 Sep 1923
Lilburn Atteberry	Iva Buck	4 Sep 1923
Steevie Edwards	Myrtle Shipley	31 Aug 1923
George Armstrong	Mrs. Mary Alvim	5 Sep 1923
Troy Carver	Minnie Edwards	7 Sep 1923
Paul Philpot	Neva McBride	30 Aug 1923
Clyde Seal	Geneva Smothers	6 Sep 1923
Hubert Grogan	Athel Luther	5 Sep 1923
Lee Apperson	Pearl Grogan	5 Sep 1923
Harvey Dunn	Lola Boswell	8 Sep 1923
Gilbert Eubanks	Cora Jones	28 Jul 1923
George Settlemoir	Hazel Dees	8 Sep 1923
Clarence Albert Palmer	Emma Marguette Salton	8 Sep 1923
Lawrence Carmickle	Ethel Johnson	25 Jul 1923
Luther May	Tessie Fiddler	14 Sep 1923
Bee Jordan	Lillian Westerfield	8 Sep 1923
W. R. Foster	Belva Roberts	19 Sep 1923
Bethel Riggs	Josie Lowery	14 Sep 1923
S. A. Hutchinson	Mattie Hammond	15 Sep 1923
Chas. Boswell	Dorothy Presley	16 Sep 1923
Leslie Little	Paralee Lynn	12 Sep 1923
Allen Prather	Ellen Keith	15 Sep 1923
Jim Pierce	Mrs. Ivena Singleton	17 Sep 1923
Kelzy Ham	Anna Belle Boyd	16 Sep 1923
Durward Whitaker	Edith Boyer	16 Sep 1923
James H. Weeks	Bessie M. Starnes	24 Sep 1923
Tobe Thompson	Lillian Ruddle	22 Sep 1923
J. M. Hammonds	Mrs. Ola Hammonds	22 Sep 1923
Bennie Lang	Mamie Baker	22 Sep 1923

GROOM	BRIDE	SOLEMNIZED
Jim Heathington	Clara Coleman	22 Sep 1923
Louie Lamb	Verdie Loftin	23 Sep 1923
T. N. Sparks	Mrs. Ella Boswell	25 Sep 1923
Harry Miller	Nora Dennington	25 Sep 1923
Lonnie Wells	Lily Creach	23 Sep 1923
Dewey Williams	Mrs. Claudie Rogers	28 Sep 1923
C. W. Mizell	Elsie Sappington	29 Sep 1923
Benjamin H. Waller	Cecil M. Hilderbrand	1 Oct 1923
J. B. Ephlin	Mrs. C. H. Hodges	3 Oct 1923
John Nelson	Caroline Jansen	30 Sep 1923
O. H. Woolard	Alice Cato	6 Oct 1923
Albert Moore	Marie Isaac	6 Oct 1923
Robert Turner	Myrtle Moore	6 Oct 1923
Arthur Edwards	Mrs. Mabel Newman	8 Oct 1923
Michael Warren	Mrs. Georgia Brown	8 Oct 1923
Paul McManus	Lena McGee	8 Oct 1923
Jesse Betts	Mrs. Thamar Letner	9 Oct 1923
Joe Edwards	Katy McManous	7 Oct 1923
T. R. Hickman	Louise Kincade	9 Oct 1923
J. O. Baledge	Rachael Wilson	10 Oct 1923
Roscoe Wells	Lela Louis	6 Oct 1923
Abe Woods	Mrs. Effie Johnson	10 Oct 1923
Charley Price	Merrill Hester	10 Oct 1923
Joe McMillian	Florine Kinder	10 Oct 1923
Bob Price	Myrtle McDaniels	9 Oct 1923
J. V. McCracken	Lillian Meddock	11 Oct 1923
J. W. Hartwick	Vessy Smith	13 Oct 1923
M. Clem	Angie Shelton	11 Oct 1923
Charley Williams	Lillie Bostwick	13 Oct 1923
Louis Belle	Louisa Cheek	13 Oct 1923
C. M. Tettaton	Nora Sutt	13 Oct 1923
Bryan Rigdon Kennedy	Pearl Brotherton	13 Oct 1923
Bonner Moore	Lillian Nesler	6 Oct 1923
Ray McGuire	Ileene Abernathy	14 Oct 1923
J. F. Anderson	Mary Rickman	15 Oct 1923
Albert Hunt	Agnes Key	14 Oct 1923
Bob Jones	Delphia Blackshire	12 Oct 1923
Clifford Basford	Septa Williams	13 Oct 1923
W. E. Sullivan	Ida B. Sullivan	13 Oct 1923
Nathan Hendley	Ollie Roland	6 Oct 1923
_. B. Arnold	Daisy Luttrell	13 Oct 1923
J. C. Lomax	Myrtle Reis	12 Oct 1923
Dee Jones	Mrs. Dena Bilderback	18 Oct 1923
Otto Hutts	Minnie Alice Nasler	15 Oct 1923

GROOM	BRIDE	SOLEMNIZED
Eli Renard (Kenard)	Ms. Martha Sexton	18 Oct 1923
Johnie Clark	Mary Brown	15 Oct 1923
Morgan Baker	Mrs. Willie Bilderback	15 Oct 1923
Ernest Davis	Myrtle Glenn	20 Oct 1923
J. F. Weaver	Thea Eller	13 Oct 1923
Ruth Wyatt	Mamie Lee Gant	20 Oct 1923
W. A. Strain	Vallie Heck	20 Oct 1923
Walter Jones	Florence Willoughby	19 Oct 1923
E. M. Moore	Martha Allen	21 Oct 1923
Robert Dover	Nora Myers	17 Oct 1923
Isaac Crouch	Mrs. Sarah Goldman	20 Oct 1923
Arthur James	Dessie Hall	20 Oct 1923
Everett V. Bolin	Lillian Tarrent	16 Oct 1923
Penny Scarbrough	Louise Bearden	21 Oct 1923
C. H. Dowler	Mrs. Mary Williams	23 Oct 1923
Chas. Renfrow	Grace Hartle	20 Oct 1923
Lennie Caldwell	Grace Hopkins	27 Oct 1923
Cecil V. Rummel	Lillian Harvey	25 Oct 1923
W. H. Mills	L. L. Nunley	3 Nov 1923
Chas. Merideth	Mrs. Myrtle Frye	7 Nov 1923
Hersel Hamlet	Elsie Kincannon	6 Nov 1923
Everett Killian	Ann Chaney	11 Nov 1923
William C. Austill	Mrs. Carrie Price	5 Nov 1923
Leroy Martin	Artie Ruth Pierce	11 Nov 1923
Milton Denton	Mrs. Pearl Owens	12 Nov 1923
Grover E. Templeton	Lula May Bray	6 Oct 1923
Elmer Jones	Mrs. Zetta Troxler	22 Sep 1923
G. W. Cox	Ethel Meadows	5 Nov 1923
Denver Smith	Bertha Jackson	3 Nov 1923
Charley Pruett	Mrs. Delia Richardson	28 Oct 1923
L. N. Proffer	Mrs. Elizabeth Tinsley	14 Oct 1923
Earl Glenn	Ida Lane	27 Oct 1923
Floyce Cross	Luella Davis	27 Oct 1923

Brodie, 77
Brooks, 74
Brotherton, 70, 84
Brown, 67-68, 74-76, 78, 81, 84-85
Brurey, 80
Bryant, 79
Brydon, 65
Bubach, 73
Buchanan, 68
Buck, 83
Buckner, 69
Bucks, 65
Bufford, 66
Bungler, 79
Burcham, 65
Burchett, 80
Burden, 76
Burgess, 75
Burk, 80
Burke, 68
Burkit, 77
Burks, 65, 67, 83
Burris, 70
Burton, 68, 71
Busby, 77
Bushong, 75
Butler, 70
Butts, 69
Byram, 79
Byrd, 71
Cabaness, 72
Cagle, 66, 68, 75-76, 82
Cain, 71
Caldwell, 77, 85
Campbell, 64, 67
Cannon, 65, 75
Capps, 64
Carmack, 73
Carmickle, 83
Carnal, 81
Carroll, 70, 73
Carry, 76
Carter, 77, 79
Carver, 83

Case, 70
Cashion, 76
Cassey, 81
Cates, 65, 82
Cato, 82, 84
Causey, 72
Cavoy, 79
Chailland, 69
Chambers, 69, 82
Chaney, 85
Chapman, 64, 79
Chatam, 76
Cheek, 84
Childers, 67-68
Childs, 73
Chilton, 79
Chism, 72
Cisco, 78
Clanin, 79
Clark, 64-65, 72, 74-76, 78, 85
Clem, 84
Clifford, 68
Clifton, 72
Clinton, 75
Cobb, 72, 76, 78, 81
Coffee, 78
Coffel, 80, 83
Coffell, 64, 73
Cole, 78
Coleman, 74-75, 83-84
Collins, 65, 70, 78-81
Colwell, 83
Common, 76
Compton, 82
Conner, 67
Conway, 69
Cook, 65, 67, 69, 71-72, 77
Cooper, 78, 83
Couch, 80
Cox, 66, 74, 80, 85
Crackel, 80
Crafford, 70
Craft, 81

Crafton, 65-66
Craig, 76
Cravens, 67
Crawford, 65-66, 77
Creach, 84
Crider, 69, 82
Crim, 65, 69
Crites, 81
Crocker, 67
Croft, 81
Cross, 69, 85
Crouch, 85
Crow, 80
Cruce, 83
Cruse, 67
Cullins, 70
Cunningham, 74, 77, 80
Curtis, 65
Daffron, 69
Daily, 73
Dample, 73
Damron, 77, 81
Darden, 71
Darenell, 75
Darnell, 77
Dartt, 76
Davenport, 67, 71, 73, 80
Davidinson, 82
Davidson, 65, 68, 71
Davis, 65, 67, 71, 73, 75, 77-79, 82-83, 85
Deck, 74, 77, 81
Dees, 83
DeLong, 82
Dement, 65
Denbow, 83
Dennington, 84
Denton, 85
Derry, 66
Derryberry, 74, 79
Devers, 70
Deycus, 74
Dickey, 81
Dickinson, 69

Granham, 69
Graves, 67, 73
Gray, 69, 85
Green, 66-67, 75
Greenfield, 73-74
Greenway, 82
Greer, 66, 78
Gregory, 68
Griffin, 64
Grimes, 64, 78
Grissom, 76
Grogan, 66, 83
Groomes, 65
Grooms, 71
Gross, 71
Grouch, 74
Grugett, 67
Guien, 66
Guillory, 64, 66
Gulley, 66
Guthrie, 75
Gwaltney, 67, 78
Hackett, 67
Hackworth, 74
Hager, 67
Haire, 80
Haislip, 65
Halder, 80
Hale, 65, 71-72
Halford, 68
Hall, 65, 68-69, 72, 85
Hallett, 73
Halley, 65
Halter, 71
Ham, 71, 78-79, 83
Hamilton, 65, 73
Hamlet, 85
Hamlin, 69
Hammond, 67, 83
Hammonds, 83
Hampton, 65-67, 70, 73, 80, 82
Hanera, 79
Haney, 75
Hanks, 78

Hannah, 70, 79
Hanners, 65
Hardy, 70
Hargraves, 78, 82
Harkey, 66, 82
Harman, 69
Harmon, 68
Harner, 79
Harp, 67
Harper, 66, 76
Harpole, 70
Harris, 66-67, 70, 75, 77, 79-80, 82
Harrison, 69, 75, 78
Hart, 66, 71, 81
Hartle, 78, 85
Hartley, 68
Hartwell, 69, 74
Hartwick, 84
Harvell, 78
Harver, 79, 81
Harvey, 85
Harwood, 74
Hatcher, 69
Hawkins, 66, 72, 81
Haycraft, 69
Hayden, 72, 78
Hays, 66-67, 80
Hearn, 66, 68
Heath, 71
Heathington, 84
Heck, 85
Hedgecock, 65
Heflin, 81
Hemphill, 64
Hendley, 84
Henry, 68
Henslee, 76
Herrell, 65, 69, 76
Herrin, 73, 77
Herrod, 68
Hester, 84
Hickman, 84
Hicks, 66, 71
Higan, 75
Higgason, 68

Higginbotham, 71
Higgins, 68
Higlen, 67
Hilderbrand, 84
Hill, 71
Hobbs, 64
Hodge, 80-81
Hodges, 68, 80, 84
Hogan, 64
Holbrook, 71
Holcomb, 74, 78
Holifield, 69
Holland, 74
Holloway, 80
Holt, 77
Homes, 79
Honnell, 70
Hood, 77
Hooper, 70
Hope, 81
Hopkins, 67-69, 79-80, 85
Horn, 80
Horner, 70, 81
Horsman, 73
Horton, 76
House, 76
Householder, 83
Houston, 71, 79
Howard, 66, 74, 76, 80, 82
Hoyclen, 73
Hubbard, 69
Hudson, 67
Huffman, 72, 74-75
Huggins, 65
Hughs, 78
Hunsaker, 73
Hunt, 84
Hunter, 66, 72
Huntsing, 82
Husband, 81
Hutchinson, 69, 81, 83
Hutton, 65
Hutts, 84

Volume 16 1923-1925

Though there are very few records for colored marriages in Dunklin County, the use of col for colored does show up a few times.

GROOM	BRIDE	SOLEMNIZED
Pertle Baird	Myrtle George	3 Nov 1923
Tom Landreth	Anna Rawlings	3 Nov 1923
William E. Scott	Pearl Brannon	3 Nov 1923
J. M. Lillard	Mrs. Sallie Owen	3 Nov 1923
Harry Thomas	Georgia Wilkins	28 Oct 1923
Albert Thomas	Myrtle Barnett	28 Oct 1923
Carl Fleeman	Ruby Tosh	27 Oct 1923
Earl Jackson	Clara Clark	29 Oct 1923
Albert Meyer	Catherine Siebert	24 Oct 1923
T. D. Hall	Mrs. Mary Floyd	31 Oct 1923
Oscar Johnson	Syble Pulley	16 Nov 1923
Rosco Wright	Addie Powell	15 Nov 1923
Bradley Stalling	Enid Vanzant	15 Nov 1923
Ross McKnight	Mrs. Hannah Baker	12 Nov 1923
George Smith	Connie Parker	17 Nov 1923
Gerald A. Ezell	Ella Brown	14 Nov 1923
Basil Ward	Ruth Anniston	8 Nov 1923
Van Woods	Flora Cole	17 Nov 1923
Lawrence Risinger	Tishie Sissom	17 Nov 1923
Levi Williams	Jewell Woods	17 Nov 1923
Oliver Myers	Gertie Riggs	29 Nov 1923
Arnold Housen	Blanch Crouch	29 Nov 1923
Arvel Daniels	Pearl Annis	11 Aug 1923
Ortie Smart	Willie Lafont	27 Nov 1923
Lyman Crites	Valley Brown	27 Nov 1923
Victor Robert Burtch	Elsie Davis	29 Nov 1923
K. G. Tinnon	Bettie Rose	28 Nov 1923
Jessie David Pritchard	Jennings Winona Huston	28 Nov 1923
Thomas Ezell	Inize Arnold	24 Nov 1923
Claudie Williams	Mrs. Ida King	3 Nov 1923
W. A. Ware	May Floyd	23 Nov 1923
Sammie Johnson	Opal Hamlett	14 Nov 1923
Ernet Doorack	Fannie Laber	21 Nov 1923
Thomas Finney	Mrs. Myrtle Fitts	13 Nov 1923
Ponder Robertson	Ruth Coleman	18 Nov 1923

GROOM	BRIDE	SOLEMNIZED
Herschel Phillips	Mrs. Bess Moore	1 Dec 1923
T. C. Ward	Lizzie Vance	1 Dec 1923
Zelmer Reeves	Carman Hardin	19 Nov 1923
John Fuller	Opal Ragsdale	17 Nov 1923
W. M. Haley (Holly)	Clara Juanita Chapple	Not Solemnized
Charley Craig	Sadie Fowler	1 Dec 1923
Ralston McCleskin (McClerkin) Wilma Lynch		21 Nov 1923
Luther Gurney Hall	Anna Louise Goodwin	21 Nov 1923
Murrel Akers	Beulah Wright	1 Dec 1923
Luther H. Triplett	Mrs. Iva M. Wright	19 Nov 1923
Charley Prater	Ida Jones	3 Nov 1923
Frank Howard	Lena Anders	10 Nov 1923
Floyd Swift	Gladys Sikes	4 Dec 1923
W. E. Mizell	Mrs. Cassie Dean	1 Nov 1923
Pledy Whitehead	Gertie Warren	2 Dec 1923
Sidney Darwood	Beatrice Petty	3 Dec 1923
Frank Followell	Pearl Russell	2 Dec 1923
M. E. Hickman	Myrtle Wadkins	8 Nov 1923
L. J. Walker	Maudie Dockins	3 Dec 1923
Homer B. Chapman	Clara Hughes	13 Nov 1923
J. D. Hughes	Mrs. Manda McCracken	1 Dec 1923
T. A. Mizell	Mrs. Ella Brannum	6 Dec 1923
Elic Johnson	Laura Kean	9 Dec 1923
A. T. Sale	Zeta Arnold	10 Dec 1923
W. R. Strickland	Lilian Silman	9 Dec 1923
E. M. Crick	Myrtle Powers	7 Dec 1923
Walter Hopper	Mrs. Emma Barnes	11 Dec 1923
John Neighbors	Ruth Cole	1 Dec 1923
Curtis Skaggs	Leona Pelts	8 Dec 1923
Roland Croom	Ilene Calfer	12 Dec 1923
Huley Howard	Leola Lines	12 Dec 1923
Charley Merritt	Electie Bayles	13 Dec 1923
Elzie Kelley	Hestella Grogen	5 Dec 1923
Luther Smith	Viola Bailey	7 Dec 1923
Loyd Brown	Katie Deblue	10 Dec 1923
Arthur Evans	Hazel Pritt	1 Dec 1923
Charley Burkett	Ailene Kinsolving	1 Dec 1923
Loyed Cook	Lorainne Odom	3 Dec 1923
Gerard Adams	Adelwa Fields	13 Dec 1923
J. F Hawkins	Emma Jewell Hallum	10 Dec 1923
Fred L. Muse	Lora M. Herrman	29 Dec 1923
A. F. Proffer	Delores Bailey	15 Dec 1923
Allie Hilton	Lena Baker	22 Dec 1923
Ben Hogland	Stella Nuckolls	30 Dec 1923

GROOM	BRIDE	SOLEMNIZED
John L. Stark	Carrie McKenzie	29 Dec 1923
Adolph Fish	Myrtle Berry	23 Dec 1923
Dawsie Baker	Morie Tanner	22 Dec 1923
Earl Shrum	Effie Hilton	22 Dec 1923
B. Osborne	Lois Osborn	26 Dec 1923
Thos. E. Crawford	Mrs. Fannie Pickens	26 Dec 1923
Melcomb Barber	Lutie May Wright	26 Dec 1923
W. C. Wilbourn	Alma Ward	26 Dec 1923
Clyde Green	Theresa Linz	28 Dec 1923
William Bradford	Lee Pearl Miles	22 Dec 1923
William A. A. Douglass	Marion C. James	23 Dec 1923
Henry R. Carroll	Jessie Hannah	27 Dec 1923
Ray Walker	Mrs. Thelma Eppihimer	24 Dec 1923
A. H. Blakemore	Bessie Smothers	24 Dec 1923
Sam Kirkman	Una Wallace	24 Dec 1923
Perry Porter	Eugenia Smith	24 Dec 1923
Ben Galvin Hedge	Mrs. Josie Moore	24 Dec 1923
Everet P. Brown	Bernice Johnson	20 Dec 1923
T. L. Young	Pearl Ray	19 Dec 1923
Ben Allen	Gertrude Moyers	22 Dec 1923
Albert Hopson	Florence Landrum	22 Dec 1923
Allen Malin	Myrtle Sturgeon	22 Dec 1923
Rube Gatewood	Lorine Kinder	22 Dec 1923
C. C. Stidham	Mrs. Minnie Taylor	9 Sep 1923
Harry Brown	Mrs. Hattie Sue Hill	16 Dec 1923
Robert Baker	Tharine Cohran (Colran,Cobron) 7 Jan 1924	
James E. Kime	Mrs. Ellen Barber	30 Dec 1923
P. A. Abernathy	Mrs. Viola Rainwater	15 Dec 1923
H. W. Winberry	Ruth Pulley	3 Jan 1924
Randy Pearman	Geneva Grooms	1 Jan 1924
Ted Hodge	Irenee Martin	4 Jan 19224
Ben F. Cook	Eva Riley	16 Dec 1923
Jasper Miller	Alma McClain	18 Dec 1923
Milton D. Kyle	Ruth Shipman	16 Dec 1923
Earl Monroe	Boodie May Dye	1 Dec 1923
Loyd Hogland	Maudie Gilbert	1 Jan 1924
David Bishop	Virgie Tidwell	31 Dec 1923
Chas. Welkey	Annie Carmickle	1 Jan 1924
W. H. Barnes	Emma D. Rush	17 Dec 1923
Jack Perry	Era Pride	20 Dec 1923
Arthur Hobbs	Gladis Barton	26 Nov 1923
Wesley Young	Agnes Oldham	14 Dec 1923
Leslie R. Hardin	Ora Hill	4 Jan 19224
Oscar Garrett	Myrtle Grass	6 Jan 1924

GROOM	BRIDE	SOLEMNIZED
Zeb Vance	Mrs. S. V. Ayres	8 Jan 1924
Frank Wineman	Rutha Lamunion	6 Jan 1924
Sidney Stewart	Florence Snider	4 Jan 19224
Welton Moore	Willie May Nations	5 Jan 1924
Roscoe Killian	Lorene Snider	4 Jan 1924
Clyde Shuttleworth	Mrs. Roberta Jones	12 Jan 1924
E. D. Campbell	Ella Bell Holder	11 Jan 1924
C. E. Sands	Charlette Malone	8 Jan 1924
Jefferson Gray	Mary Wiliby	3 Jan 1924
E. J. Sanders	Lizzie McNeal	8 Jan 1924
Glennis Hopwood	Josephine Rittenberry	8 Jan 1924
J. T. Beeman	Bashie Green	9 Feb 1924
C. T. McNeill	Banner Luther	26 Jan 1924
J. R. Walker	Mrs. Mattie Proffer	9 Feb 1924
Oscar Landreth	Lottie Justice	1 Feb 1924
Chas. Miller	Ida Rideout	31 Jan 1924
Roy Hubbard	Mrs. Millie Kelly	9 Feb 1924
Alfred Nally	Gertie Esterline	9 Feb 1924
Oscar Meek	Lola James	8 Feb 1924
B. H. Kennon	Dollie C. Blankenship	3 Feb 1924
Mark Allen	May Walker	3 Feb 1924
Izieare Valentine	Florence Eldonia Manley	31 Jan 1924
W. W. Gordon	Lieninda Gaines	17 Jan 1924
Bob Horner	Emma Ferguson	2 Feb 1924
Thos. J. Crim	Mrs. Florence Hicks	2 Feb 1924
Elmer Kelly	Dorothy Grimes	1 Feb 1924
Ben Portwood	Genevieve Singleton	2 Feb 1924
Egbert West	Agness Bounds	1 Feb 1924
W. T. Smith	Minnie B. Key	26 Jan 1924
Louie Nail	Hazel Cartwright	19 Jan 1924
Eugene Vermillion	Mrs. Minnie Williams	11 Jan 1924
Lotton Phillips	Dovie Hart	25 Jan 1924
Wilburn Cullins	Bessie May Matthews	26 Jan 1924
W. T. Franks	Bessie Grimes	28 Jan 1924
Connie D. Trobaugh	Letea Holifield	13 Jan 1924
Sam Willard	Gladys Willard	16 Feb 1924
Roy Wineman	Nell Spoulding	16 Feb 1924
Elmer R. Stephens	Clara Mangold	16 Feb 1924
A. A. Magonick	Susie Smith	14 Feb 1924
E. R. Julian	Anna Hamilton	27 Feb 1924
Willie Hammon	Ethel Dehart	13 Feb 1924
Claud Hamilton	Rena Jordan	24 Jan 1924
Roy Smith	Maggie Gunter	3 Jan 1924
J. M. Armour	Mrs. L. A. Earnst	22 Jan 1924

GROOM	BRIDE	SOLEMNIZED
Raymond Wadley	Ethel Marie Vandiver	21 Jan 1924
Everett Vandiver	Gladys Calahan	21 Jan 1924
Miles A. Floyd	Beatress Tu___	21 Jan 1924
H. L. Coley	Nola May Psalmonds	20 Jan 1924
S. F. Goodrich	Mrs. Susie Davis	16 Jan 1924
Otis Herrell	Martha Halbrook	21 Jan 1924
Frank Swanner	Lola Gaskins	20 Jan 1924
Lynn Bethel	Pansey Singleton	19 Jan 1924
Silas Newman	Maud Albright	18 Jan 1924
Richard Roberts	Minnie Lee	16 Jan 1924
Namoen Myers	Oma (Orna) Penrod	25 Nov 1923
Samuel L. Dunaway	Beulah Kirkman	23 Jan 1924
Enos Carpenter	May Wilson	26 Jan 1924
Fred Duncan	Sadie Winberry	25 Jan 1924
C. E. Gaddis	Mrs. Lula George	28 Jan 1924
Willie Dobin	Ruthie Jackson	22 Jan 1924
Elmer Ferren	Elva McFadden	23 Feb 1924
W. M. English	Francis Warren	21 Feb 1924
W. G. Osborne	Francis Hamilton	21 Feb 1924
Louis Pope	Opel Oakes	20 Feb 1924
Harvey O'neal	Ethel Lasswell	29 Feb 1924
P. P. Hensley	Mrs. Mary A. Moore	1 Mar 1924
L. M. Willman	Lena L. Hickerson	26 Feb 1924
Chas. Atchley	Josephine Kent	1 Mar 1924
Clyde Tarrant	Thelma Kimbrow	12 Feb 1924
Clarence Swartz	Eva George	20 Feb 1924
J. W. Willman	Ada Keys	11 Feb 1924
E. T. Smith	Udilla Harrison	12 Feb 1924
Harvey Walthers	Aggie Noble	24 Feb 1924
Harry Jackson	Mrs. Clara May Smith	27 Feb 1924
W. M. Neely	Lois Middleton	18 Feb 1924
George Harwell	Dovie Dickerson	2 Mar 1924
Jim Franklin	Annabell Marshall	6 Mar 1924
Ralph Glasgow	Opal Riddle	28 Feb 1924
Edgar Clay	Myrtle Lasswell	3 Mar 1924
Curtis Sawyers	Pearline Fields	28 Feb 1924
Louis Hulen	Mrs. Effie Nelson	2 Mar 1924
Harvey Austin	Belle Lasswell	2 Mar 1924
Thos. W. Lancaster	Myrtle Mann	7 Mar 1924
W. A. Gordon	Mrs. Idona Richardson	8 Mar 1924
E. L. King	Mildred Irene Henry	8 Mar 1924
Walter A. Baker	Celia E. Baker	4 Mar 1924
Marion Wren	Ruby Clemons	9 Mar 1924
Clarence Nail	Sadie Williams	15 Mar 1924

GROOM	BRIDE	SOLEMNIZED
C. R. Young	Mrs. Violet Crawford	14 Mar 1924
J. H. Pettijohn	Lillian Craig	10 Mar 1924
W. A. Demay	Flora Smothers	13 Mar 1924
Elmer Carter	Elsie Keaton	21 Mar 1924
E. K. Killbreth	Mrs. Nettie Shou__	1 Mar 1924
J. C. Ridley	Mrs. Maggie Edwards	17 Mar 1924
Clark Saller	Bell Barham	16 Feb 1924
O. L. Vincent	Mrs. Edna Johnson	20 Mar 1924
Willie Maben	Margaret Durden	16 Mar 1924
C. J. Johnson	Amy Louis	8 Mar 1924
Orestes H. Graaf	Mary Lee Pollock	16 Mar 1924
W. O. Malin	Maggie Peace	22 Mar 1924
Frank A. Hemmer	Lareane Geist	13 Mar 1924
Jesse C. Sheehy	Dorothy Johnson	20 Mar 1924
E. W. Brown	Mrs. Nettie Brown	18 Mar 1924
Ernest Bachelor	Cara Cackel	23 Mar 1924
G. W. Herrell	Ida Cato	23 Mar 1924
Webb Thornton	Ada Grubb	23 Mar 1924
Earl Ray	Dona Malin	25 Mar 1924
M. L. Stone	Mary A. Williamson	1 Jan 1924
H. R. Bankston	Mrs. Snoda Baker	29 Mar 1924
Sam Hart	Viola Tuck	31 Apr (Mar) 1924
W. H. Adams	Julia Cunningham	7 Apr 1924
William McCloud	Mamie Bess	1 Apr 1924
Eugene Williams	Anna Pearl Peacher	5 Apr 1924
E. C. Chambers	Stella Cook	4 Apr 1924
George Wolf	Arie Roach	11 Apr 1924
R. A. Adkins	Martha Pruett	30 Mar 1924
Ray H. Baum	Ruth Foster	2 Apr 1924
Frank Baker	Bessie McLeskey	29 Mar 1924
Clifton Dunn	Emaline Ginn	15 Apr 1924
Frank Haywood	Bessie Side	13 Apr 1924
Joe Burnett	Lilly May Stark	15 Apr 1924
J. W. Boatwright Jr.	Clara Furry	19 Apr 1924
Roy J. Cope	Carnelia Corder	20 Apr 1924
J. H. Snipes	Mrs. Addie Collins	26 Apr 1924
Albert G. Feldmann	Aeonora B. Fielder	23 Apr 1924
E. A. Mitchell	Pearl Joyner	20 Apr 1924
Everett McKinzie	Samantha Shepard	22 Apr 1924
J. W. Washington	Mrs. Lucille Bronson	28 Apr 1924
Louis Ball	Ida May Blackmon	30 Apr 1924
William Tucker	Eula Moore	1 May 1924
William W. Turner	Ola Barber	30 Apr 1924
James O. Casey	Pearl Fitzpatrick	4 May 1924

GROOM	BRIDE	SOLEMNIZED
Lonnie Tanner	Mrs. Lydnie Ivy	4 May 1924
Archie Wilson	Opal Wilson	1 May 1924
Walter E. Jolly	Florence Wall	15 May 1924
Arthur James	Dewesa Neice	4 May 1924
Arthur Layton	Eva Chambers	13 May 1924
Marcus Wells	Roena Wildman	10 May 1924
Ed Davis	Julie Mager	10 May 1924
Ray Yeargain	Ethel Nolen	10 May 1924
Elmer Goble	Rilla Maddox	12 May 1924
Willie Elliott	Ollie Waddell	10 May 1924
W. T. Ramond	Beatrice Whitehead	10 May 1924
D. V. Wicker	Ruth Hicks	26 Apr 1924
George Hardyman	Thelma Cook	8 May 1924
Jeff Mason	Mattie Rauls	7 May 1924
Jewell Chipman	Ruby Bohannon	16 May 1924
Hugh H. Foster	Betty Maud Donaldson	14 May 1924
William Cox	Dorris Butcher	29 Mar 1924
Jennings West	Reba Jeffords	20 May 1924
R. T. Lebo	W. H. Barham	15 May 1924
Zalmer Kitchell	Cordy Ruth Mitchell	4 May 1924
Boss(Bass) Mitchell	Icy Mason	2 May 1924
Willie Hodges	Sylvia Cobb	4 May 1924
A. Z. Joiner	Flora J. Kitchell	4 May 1924
Earl Waddley	Cordelia White	11 May 1924
Mack Young	Annie Cantrill	14 May 1924
Earl Shelton	Mary F. Redman	25 May 1924
Adam Thompson	Darthal Thompson	26 May 1924
Harry N. Keith	Bertha A. Russell	30 May 1924
David E. Wood	Miami B. Lusk	31 May 1924
Charley Craig	Anna Wilkerson	1 Jun 1924
Howard Farrar	Delia Wilson	1 Jun 1924
Neely C. Binkley	Elsie Weatherholt	31 May 1924
Charlie Hudgins	Georgia Weatherspoon	29 May 1924
T. J. Griffin	Mary M. Wilson	5 Jun 1924
Floyd Harvey	Mattie Brown	3 Jun 1924
Howard Lane	Naomi Braden	30 May 1924
Bert Shaffer	Ethel Dellinger	7 Jun 1924
J. R. Owens	Hattie Cawthon	14 May 1924
Frank Green	Parley Marler	17 Jun 1924
Emery Griggs	Augusta Wilkins	19 Jun 1924
Simmon May	Susie Chandler	19 Jun 1924
Clifford Dye	Rose Blanchard	15 Jun 1924
Ephraim Maglothin	Opal Holifield	21 Jun 1924

GROOM	BRIDE	SOLEMNIZED
Arthur Massey	Marine Lewis	21 Jun 1924
B. T. Wells	Mary Johnson	22 Jun 1924
J. B. Sutton	Matilda Jackson	14 Jun 1924
Frank Jones	Lola Deenes	26 Jun 1924
Norman E. Dunscomb	Martha N. Heinlen	23 Jun 1924
Virgil Hale	Isabel Mansfield	12 Jul 1924
Otis Bryan Welker	Mrs. Pearl Looney	12 Jul 1924
Allie Edmonston	Mrs. Eva Crane	16 Jul 1924
Lawrence M. Pickering	Beulah Snider	15 Jul 1924
Dayton Ham	Hester Palmer	4 Jul 1924
O. E. Bledsoe	Ella Hatfield	5 Jul 1924
Earl Howard	Lillian Thornton	28 Jun 1924
C. E. Leatherman	Mrs. Lizzie Burton	14 Jul 1924
W. R. Sheppard	Mrs. Mattie M. Holt	12 Jul 1924
Otto Austin	Ada Neeley	8 Jul 1924
Henry Range	Georgia Franklin	5 Jul 1924
Charley Oden	Madge Alford	14 Jul 1924
B. C. Taylor	Ruth Brannon	5 Jul 1924
C. D. Hill	Annie Burrows	5 Jul 1924
Lonzo Sykes	Rosalee Deen	6 Jul 1924
Frank Jones	Dollie Range	22 Jun 1924
Joe Folston	Mrs. Hattie Thomas	10 Jul 1924
George Fleeman Hemphill	Irene Baldwin	16 Jul 1924
George James	Sadie Holt	5 Jul 1924
Jack Morgan	Marie Walker	9 Jul 1924
Fred Riddle	Adene Melcher	18 Jul 1924
Earl Walthers	Bertha Davis	17 Jul 1924
John B. Thomassen	Hanna Bell McGee	21 Jul 1924
Ernest Kinchen	Julia Taylor	3 Jul 1924
G. C. Foster	Gracie James	21 Jul 1924
Jake Thompson	Jessie Pullins	18 Jul 1924
E. A. Rodermund	Mrs. Delia Parker	5 Aug 1924
Robert L. Smith	Georgia Etta McNeal	18 Aug 1924
Mack (Mark) Seals	May Haythorn	2 Aug 1924
Ray Birchfield	Anna Stockton	8 Aug 1924
Chas. E. Price	Mrs. Francis Skelton	10 Aug 1924
Jake Cullum	Julia Lee	3 Aug 1924
General Govand	Flora Richardson	11 Aug 1924
Sip Knox	Jessie Hopkins	31 Jul 1924
W. T. Caneer	Bertha Bryant	6 Aug 1924
H. W. Keen	Delia Bowman	24 Jul 1924
T. S. Melton	Birdie Ensley	16 Aug 1924
C. R. Dunlap	B. R. Edmonds	16 Aug 1924
Jack Lord	Beatrice Biggs	17 Aug 1924

GROOM	BRIDE	SOLEMNIZED
Robert F. Love	Nillie Henderson	19 Aug 1924
Harry McNew	Ruthy Batchelor	1 Aug 1924
Earl Rose	Lora Pullin	27 Aug 1924
James Robinson	Mrs. Vertie Brown	7 Jul 1924
Cicero C. Capshaw	Mrs. Lucy M. Young	22 Jul 1924
John H. Holmes	Mrs. Georgia Winbers	13 Jul 1924
W. H. Hart	Edna Davis	24 Jul 1924
B. W. Nanney	Dulah Honeycut	19 Aug 1924
Henry Taylor	Rosa Lee	18 Aug 1924
Herbert Ray	Opal M. Parker	10 Aug 1924
J. W. Mandrell	Mrs. Rosa Dudley	19 Jun 1924
Ivey Reagon	Beatrice Churchwell	10 Aug 1924
Monroe Adams	Bettie Hurston	15 Aug 1924
William Berry	Ruth Brooks	20 Jul 1924
Harry Richardson	Mollie Parker	1 Aug 1924
Curtis Crawford	Zeddie Shoemaker	2 Aug 1924
Floyd Smothers	Ivy McCombs	29 Jul 1924
Bennie Lambert	Gay Greer	19 Aug 1924
James Stephens	Ida Tinker	20 Aug 1924
Nute Strickland	Beatrice Turner	23 Aug 1924
T. D. Denon	Elsie Hubbard	23 Aug 1924
Edward Adolph	Beatrice Eubanks	23 Aug 1924
J. M. Duffle	Norah McGill	24 Aug 1924
William D. Howe	Mittie Cason	23 Aug 1924
J. R. Horseman	Mrs. Lona Vails	23 Aug 1924
J. O. Long	Lena Gunels	26 Aug 1924
Lawrence Carral	Mrs. Ottis Minor	23 Aug 1924
W. D. Montgomery	Carie Briggs	26 Aug 1924
Homer Waxler	Virginia French	30 Aug 1924
B. A. Goodrich	Mrs. Alice Pruett	31 May 1924
J. C. Miller	Alma Dailey	5 Aug 1924
Tom Tankersley	Mrs. Jannie Emerson	30 Aug 1924
Loyd Butler	Kittie Litchford	30 Aug 1924
Frank Greenfield	Flora Bell Mooneham	2 Sep 1924
William Green	Mrs. May Marvel	29 Aug 1924
Abb Greenville	Mrs. Emma Hughes	1 Sep 1924
Herbert Hutchinson	Annie Pennington	4 Sep 1924
W. A. Holbrook	Ruth Graham	22 Aug 1924
Lawrence A. Myrick	Lillian Irene Lewis	27 Aug 1924
Wm. Caine	Fannie Chaise	31 Aug 1924
Robert Jones	Virgie Maples	3 Sep 1924
Loyce Newman	Katherine Legon	7 Sep 1924
Shelby Hubbell	Mrs. Genetta Fisher	6 Sep 1924
Kelly Mullen	Cora Lincoln	10 Sep 1924

GROOM	BRIDE	SOLEMNIZED
Douglas Mauser	Ethel Bowles	9 Sep 1924
Arthur E. Petty	Rosie E. Crow	30 Aug 1924
Mack (Mark) Wallace	Norah Stackhouse	10 Sep 1924
J. O. Cates	Dollie Gilliam	7 Sep 1924
Elmer Tate	Annie Smallwood	5 Sep 1924
W. H. McDaniel	Mrs. Sybil Austin	14 Sep 1924
Ernest Langford	Mable Hurt	16 Sep 1924
D. W. Baldridge	Hannah Leggon	14 Sep 1924
Jennings Snider	Fannie Pennington	20 Sep 1924
W. M. Lowry	Mamie Wallace	22 Sep 1924
Earl Lockland	Pearl Clemons	18 Sep 1924
Logan Harris	Edna Pratt	18 Sep 1924
Morris Wilson	Cemmie Williams	21 Sep 1924
Oscar Wells	Etta Tilley	11 Sep 1924
Alvia Burkes	Bessie Forbes	27 Sep 1924
Frank McCain	Anna Insco	25 Sep 1924
Otto Isbell	Dollie Halloway	26 Sep 1924
Matt Walls	Mary J. Weldon	28 Sep 1924
Ollie R. Coates	Mary Coats	29 Sep 1924
Isaac T. Brown	Mrs. Rachel Shelton	30 Sep 1924
Setch Meriel	Henriett Kibler	30 Sep 1924
L. S. Barger	Mrs. Francis Tally	19 Sep 1924
Lilbren Thompson	Iva Jordon	3 Oct 1924
Dant Dempsey	Mrs. Ethel Freeman	1 Oct 1924
Willie McKnight	Anna Branch	4 Oct 1924
Sivie Price	Helen Robinson	4 Oct 1924
Dewer Brown	Gladys Kirby	4 Oct 1924
Noble Hurt	Lovenia Mangrum	4 Oct 1924
J. A. Sandefur	Mattie Ryan	13 Oct 1924
Elmer James	Atlas McNeal	11 Oct 1924
Charley Edminston	Dona White	12 Oct 1924
J. H. Burgess	Ruth Young	11 Oct 1924
Jack Scott	Viola Hart	14 Oct 1924
Willard Sisk	Pearlie Dubar	4 Oct 1924
Joe Wilson	Thelma Thornberry	14 Oct 1924
Edgar Wilson	Ruth Thornberry	14 Oct 1924
J. W. Shipman	Cora Williams	5 Oct 1924
Alvin Reagan	Clady Pitts	4 Oct 1924
Ray Maples	Ethel Tucker	2 Oct 1924
Cecil Morrow	Belva Dehart	5 Oct 1924
C. E. Summitt	Arena Burcham	3 Oct 1924
Archie Williams	Edith Loftin	4 Oct 1924
Willie Prince	Mrs. Rachel Harkey	5 Oct 1924
Ira McNew	Zaie Warren	8 Oct 1924

GROOM	BRIDE	SOLEMNIZED
W. M. Moore	Alma Eaker	9 Oct 1924
Jessie Ferguson	Catherine Crawford	7 Oct 1924
Luther Chapman	Mrs. Dovie Stafford	5 Oct 1924
Robert Yeargen	Estel Dubar	9 Oct 1924
V. Barnes	Maud Taylor	8 Oct 1924
Fred Moore	Lola May Strawn	10 Oct 1924
George G. Miller	Georgia Opal Dearing	10 Oct 1924
Chas. A. Middlersworth	Emma Partridge	7 Aug 1924
Claud Lozier	Lizzie Thrasher	17 Oct 1924
Allen Johnson	Lula Prince	19 Oct 1924
J. C. Little	Mrs. Nettie May Harrington	22 Oct 1924
Roy Hedgcock	Ruth Jones	11 Oct 1924
A. L. Dunning	Esthel Austion	27 Oct 1924
Ernest Stallions	Edna Blaze	25 Oct 1924
Louis Hill	Adeline Norris	25 Oct 1924
J. H. Anderson	Susie Coleman	25 Oct 1924
Homer Johnson	Gertrude Carr	25 Oct 1924
E. L. Landrum	Bertha E. Perry	18 Oct 1924
Cecil Smith	Ella Mansell	25 Oct 1924
Tollie Battles	Mrs. Flora Blankenship	29 Oct 1924
R. A. Young	Hattie Ezell	29 Oct 1924
M. E. Wright	Mrs. Ada Noble	27 Oct 1924
Chas. Marler	Mrs. Pearlie Belle Causey	26 Oct 1924
L. F. Dunn	Mrs. Mary Pickett	25 Oct 1924
Matt L. Love	Callie Wimms	5 Oct 1924
A. C. McFall	Francis Elizabeth Goodrich	15 Oct 1924
Clifford Wilborn	Rachel Owens	13 Sep 1924
Clifford Walker	Myrtle Frailey	1 Nov 1924
Sherman Fulkerson	Ethen Snider	1 Nov 1924
F. R. Davenport	Amanda Hodge	31 Oct 1924
LaFate Morris	Nellie Carnie	1 Nov 1924
Morris Right	Willie Frenchman	15 Oct 1924
Henry Clark	Margaret Dennis	15 Oct 1924
Earl Caly	Lacy Turner	26 Oct 1924
Walter Allen	Hattie Singleton	7 Nov 1924
J. C. Thomas	Mrs. Nellie B. Rodehever	7 Nov 1924
Lawrence Daniel	Laura Jackson	8 Nov 1924
S. P. Osborn	Mrs. Jennie Burkhart	12 Nov 1924
Luther Williams	Edna Houchins	12 Nov 1924
Walter L. Harper	Lora Pelts	8 Nov 1924
Dallas Slaughter	Viola Robertson	6 Nov 1924
Oscar Johnson	Bertha Tash	8 Nov 1924
Tommy Burks	Lizzie Hicks	10 Nov 1924
William A. Clingingsworth	Alace Mills	2 Nov 1924

GROOM	BRIDE	SOLEMNIZED
Tom Eskew	Mrs. Pearl Tucker	20 Nov 1924
Eddie Branch	Janie Cora Hampton	15 Nov 1924
Willie Walls	Rheulane Manes	14 Nov 1924
Jim Jackson	Mrs. Lottie Hodge	14 Nov 1924
Chester Duncan	Mildred Dees	15 Nov 1924
Earl Cash	Mrs. Bessie Dillon	15 Nov 1924
L. A. Johnson	Mrs. Julia Rose	15 Nov 1924
F. W. Jenkins	Rosey Phillips	19 Nov 1924
D. E. Evans	Mrs. M. T. Husketh	20 Nov 1924
L. H. Logon	Mrs. Minnie McCombs	20 Nov 1924
George Easley	Florence Walker	17 Nov 1924
Virgil Moore	Parralee Jones	17 Nov 1924
J. A. Julian	Ethel May Wallace	22 Nov 1924
Luther Ayres	Elvia Sigers	25 Nov 1924
Raymond L. Jones	Vesta Lanier	28 Nov 1924
Thomas Burchett	Cora Strap	30 Nov 1924
Lewis Crews	Mary Murrell	8 Dec 1924
D. V. Moore	Orna B. Farmer	8 Dec 1924
H. E. Rayburn	Kettie Capshaw	14 Dec 1924
Max Pruett	Pauline Cagle	13 Dec 1924
George Wilson	Blanch Allan Mitchell	16 Dec 1924
Walter White	Mrs. Nellie Biggs	15 Dec 1924
Albert Motley	Mrs. Cinderella Jones	13 Dec 1924
W. T. Tidwell	Rose Robinson	13 Dec 1924
Howard Taylor	Luzenia Rouse	13 Dec 1924
Z. W. Parr	Flora Churchwell	19 Nov 1924
Clyde Gibbs	Sylvia Ray	6 Dec 1924
R. E. Wells	Mrs. Clara Crow	7 Dec 1924
Howard Barnes	Florence Sutton	10 Dec 1924
C. H. Martin	Emma Louisa Taylor	7 Dec 1924
Bill Stokes	Mrs. Elsie Gammons	6 Dec 1924
Henry Shaw	Lorine Rogers	8 Dec 1924
John Glenn	Jewell Carter	6 Dec 1924
Allen Marchbanks	Louise Norman	6 Dec 1924
J. M. Bassinger	Mary Blevings	3 Dec 1924
William Vass (Voss)	Birdie Hester	6 Dec 1924
F. M. Lacy	Mary Agness Stinebrook	3 Dec 1924
Clarence Morris	Mrs. Helen Anderson	3 Dec 1924
C. J. Kinser	Mrs. Dovey Watson	30 Nov 1924
H. P. Hardy	Mrs. Sarah Adkins	30 Nov 1924
Fidelis Becker	Edith Vander_oseh	26 Nov 1924
Leonard Albertson	Hassie Edwards	29 Nov 1924
Robert Davenport	Effic Lovings	28 Nov 1924
R. B. Miles	Mrs. Lela Diggs	29 Nov 1924

GROOM	BRIDE	SOLEMNIZED
Joe Ford	Lottie Gee	7 Dec 1924
Harry Dawson	Jennie Herrin	20 Dec 1924
Charley McCray	Lucy May Reddick	13 Dec 1924
Fred Coleman	Rachel Richardson	22 Dec 1924
Harry Ray	Lorna Hargis	30 Nov 1924
Kemp Money	Edna Watson	17 Dec 1924
G. W. Parrent	Mrs. Celia Sutton	24 Dec 1924
Lee Switzer	Mrs. Bertha Bullins (Pullins)	24 Dec 1924
Roy Stanley	Hazel Hurst	24 Dec 1924
J. R. Williams	Mamie Patton	24 Dec 1924
Earl Voss	Ruby Riggs	25 Dec 1924
H. D. Diggs	Rhoda E. Matthews	24 Dec 1924
Tom Herrell	Gladys Bassinger	25 Dec 1924
Pink Herrell	Mrs. Dicey Graham	25 Dec 1924
Thos. H. Polsgrove	Mrs. Ellen Shell	24 Dec 1924
T. L. Warren	Mary Cross	30 Dec 1924
G. W. Davis	Lucy Sherrod	29 Dec 1924
C. M. Robertson	Nettie Trout	1 Jan 1925
E. J. Cook	Berah Crutchfield	31 Dec 1924
Nolen Watson	Regina Roberts	1 Jan 1925
Clarence A. Green	Pearl Banthrall	3 Jan 1925
Tom Massey	Annie Britt	28 Dec 1924
W. S. Blakemore	Lena Pritchard	25 Dec 1924
Clinton Neely	Mrs. Lexie Smith	5 Jan 1925
Glenn B. Sundy (Lundy)	Pauline Douglass	29 Dec 1924
Willie Ringold	Willie Collins	29 Dec 1924
Coleman Kelley	Laura Williams	28 Dec 1924
L. M. Cupp	Mrs. Orna (Oma) Gatlin	27 Dec 1924
E. A. Stacy Jr.	Mrs. Zoe Stacy	6 Jan 1925
Ronnel Johnson	Grace Mattics	9 Jan 1925
Simon McNeil	Julia Boyd	10 Jan 1925
Andrew Holmes	Bethel Mayes	18 Jan 1925
Charles Chamberlain	Emma Moore	17 Jan 1925
Walice Tucker	Aluetta Lester	3 Jan 1925
Will Moore	Ninner Thompson	25 Dec 1924
Ody Edgin	Mary Gibson	17 Jan 1925
Guy Grant	Ossie Smith	17 Jan 1925
Dennis Thomas	Madge Lane	11 Jan 1925
Calvin C. Fuller	Mary Melvina Steinbridge	11 Jan 1925
Milton Robinson	Vira Dale	14 Jan 1925
Carl Lemonds	Madeline Long	10 Jan 1925
John Collins	Lucy Paris	19 Jan 1925
Ernest B. Benline (Berline)	Alma Berry	17 Jan 1925
Roosevelt Goolesby	Velma Conaway	21 Jan 1925

GROOM	BRIDE	SOLEMNIZED
S. A. Cannon	Mrs. Maudy McGraw	22 Jan 1925
R. E. Bailey	Selma Gilcrist	20 Aug 1924
Hilton Morris	Ruth Mitchell	25 Jan 1925
Jim Abbott	Ethel Landers	24 Jan 1925
J. R. Beardsley	Mrs. Annie Stokes	22 Jan 1925
Elzie McCallom	Alma Brown	24 Jan 1925
Alvin Lewis	Willie Cook	24 Jan 1925
Charlie Edwin Stokes	Sarah Selby Culbertson	24 Jan 1925
Truman E. Wood	Mrs. Daisy May Hill	24 Jan 1925
W. M. Scott	Flossie Greenway	21 Jan 1925
Nelson Luckday	Julia Woods	29 Jan 1925
H. C. Cook	Lola Yount	10 Jan 1925
J. O. Dodd	Lena Walls (Wells)	21 Dec 1924
Chas. Parish	Letha Yow	29 Jan 1925
Tom Skinner	Louella Blount	23 Jan 1925
Raymond Manasio	Edna Odel	31 Jan 1925
Otis Clyde Dallas	Gracie Marguerite Price	31 Jan 1925
E. F. Foresyth	Clara Switzer	31 Jan 1925
Wilson Jarvis	Myrtle Rosenbum	25 Nov 1924
Reyford Pollard	Agnes Smithwick	8 Oct 1924
W. D. Simpson	Ollie B. Dempsey	1 Feb 1925
J. D. Johnson	Mrs. L. P. Shirell	26 Jan 1925
D. L. Langley	Mrs. Cora Smith	31 Jan 1925
Lawrence J. Yahl	Margaret A. Polys	4 Feb 1925
Raymond Crawley	Lois Veatch	6 Feb 1925
A. W. Fowler	Willie Carter	14 Feb 1925
John Moore	Henrette McCauley	22 Feb 1925
W. D. Felker	Florence Fields	24 Jan 1925
Bill Drake	Nora Stacy	18 Feb 1925
G. W. Dean	Mrs. Sudie Flowers	17 Feb 1925
T. J. Bohannon	Mrs. Grace Hull	8 Feb 1925
Leonard Little	Della Braden	8 Feb 1925
James Ross	Ethel Starks	7 Feb 1925
Charles Hull	Lizzie Morgan	2 Feb 1925
Holley A. Bankston	Edna Bush	5 Feb 1925
Otto Bean	Alice Lee	26 Jan 1925
Paul Mancell	Lula James	7 Feb 1925
Ora Conran	Beulah Reel	4 Feb 1925
Earl Midgett	Irene Head	10 Feb 1925
James T. Whitehouse	Della Story	21 Feb 1925
Martin Kinzey	Jessie Turbeville	24 Feb 1925
H. A. Jones	Roy Ellen Stewart	30 Jan 1925
Jim Wallis	Myrtle Shirley	16 Feb 1925
Henry Cooper	Mrs. Priscilla Pendleton	22 Feb 1925

GROOM	BRIDE	SOLEMNIZED
Henry Lewis	Mattie Reed	17 Feb 1925
Ervin Hatcher	Lucille Farmer	21 Feb 1925
Roy Green	Susie Fortune	21 Feb 1925
George Smith	Iva Jennings	14 Feb 1925
Frank Irvin	Hallie Harris	14 Feb 1925
Martin W. Howard	Fay Bernice Napper	20 Feb 1925
Charles Henry Feldmann	Genevieve Elizabeth Vanderbosch	24 Feb 1925
Berl Chase	Mildred Cleveland	28 Feb 1925
N. B. Langley	Arthur Lee Robertson	16 Feb 1925
Ezra Smith	Zora Blanchard	28 Feb 1925
Elmer Reese	Gladys Clubb	21 Feb 1925
C. C. Gray	Elvia Huffman	28 Feb 1925
John Robinson	Anna Parkin	21 Feb 1925
Charley Kirby	Effie Thrasher	2 Mar 1925
Alvie Bunting	Gertie Crawford	28 Feb 1925
S. W. Curry	Mrs. Kate Finley	28 Feb 1925
Richard Swank	Florence Tippitt	2 Mar 1925
Clyde Goodwin	Lillie Jones	28 Feb 1925
T. A. Dean	Hattie Smith	5 Mar 1925
Ellick Jones	Dollie Hampton	1 Mar 1925
S. T. Forest (Foust)	Dollie Meatte	5 Mar 1925
Winford Rather	Dora Wright	7 Mar 1925
Arthur Young	Emma McClain	7 Mar 1925
O. H. Noble	JoAnnie Williams	3 Mar 1925
J. M. Benton	Janie George	21 Jan 1925
Elmer T. Brunt	Alma Lou Neel	9 Mar 1925
Fred Douglass	Anna Brown	1 Mar 1925
And (Aud) Smith	Pearl Holder	14 Mar 1925
Truman Smith	Beulah Cooper	7 Mar 1925
Andrew Woodson	Lue Howard	27 Feb 1925
Orval Craig	Myrtle Killian	26 Mar 1925
Martin Masterson	Roma Harvey	14 Mar 1925
Guy Crosk	Rebecca Elmore	23 Mar 1925
John Leslie Clemson	Ruth C. Buck	21 Mar 1925
Millard Patrick	Ethel Crawley	28 Mar 1925
Will Lacy	Minnie Davis	28 Mar 1925
Asa Ledbetter	Lizzie Aburshan	28 Mar 1925
Oscar Genter	Mable Schuhmache	28 Mar 1925
J. C. Gabriel	Millie Henfling	29 Mar 1925
Eugene Farless	Dovy Dillingham	24 Mar 1925
R. S. McDonald	Celine Elam	5 Apr 1925
Joe Emanuel Jr.	Beulah McCain	6 Apr 1925
W. H. Wheeler	Ola Glenn	1 Mar 1925
Eura Edmonds	Dovie Michie	21 Jan 1925

GROOM	BRIDE	SOLEMNIZED
Robert Frields	Mrs. Marie Hughes	2 Apr 1925
H. B. Burton	Mrs. L. A. fiddler	3 Apr 1925
Hubert Reagon	Mrs. Annie Gibson	3 Apr 1925
D. L. Moore	Mrs. Lucy Cook	6 Apr 1925
Bud Anderson	Eunice Mitchell	11 Apr 1925
Theodore Vance	Maybell Bridges	9 Apr 1925
Lee Flowers	Louise Todd	12 Apr 1925
Sam Biggs	Malinda Jane Calhoun	13 Apr 1925
F. B. Stephens	Della Walls	11 Apr 1925
Enoch Floyd	Lillie Massey	13 Apr 1925
Fred Barber	Madge Gregson	13 Apr 1925
Joe Moore	Stella George	18 Apr 1925
Wright McNeal	Lizand Thomas	8 Apr 1925
G. C. Portwood	Mrs. Lora Gore	11 Apr 1925
Searcy L. Taylor	Thesa Lee Traylor	18 Apr 1925
Arthur Forrester	Elsie Corn (Coon)	22 May 1925
Belton B. Sharp	Rosa Lee Turner	20 May 1925
John Lutes	Goldie Rogers	17 May 1925
W. G. Vancleve	Louis Wells	19 May 1925
W. F. Shelton Jr.	Ruby Smith	16 May 1925
Claude Tidwell	Mrs. Evan Shepard	8 Jun 1925
James Washington	Mrs. Loraine Parker	28 Mar 1925
Earl Boyer	Pearl Doyel	23 Apr 1925
Cedel Bonaby	Pearlie Johnson	20 Apr 1925
David R. Rogers	Flora B. Bester	27 Apr 1925
R. D. Hormer (Horner)	Opal Rhew	29 Apr 1925
J. H. Nipper	Pood Cuff	1 May 1925
F. A. Michels	Fredeth Pearson	5 May 1925
Louis Maffett	Mrs. Emma Collins	17 Apr 1925
William L. Elliott	Nannie J. Hampton	4 May 1925
Mitchell Crawford	Hettie Davis	11 May 1925
Lewis Lowery	Elva Akridge	11 May 1925
Albert R. Flippin	Mrs. Lela Williams	3 May 1925
P. H. Andrews	Susie Tyler	3 May 1925
Otto Shirrell	Pearl White	9 May 1925
Nathan Wilson	Anna Woolums	22 Apr 1925
C. C. Wofford	Ella Frie	1 Mar 1925
Harry Gooch	Easter Rogers	6 May 1925
Hubert Johnson	May Duffey	30 Apr 1925
J. R. Eagle	Mrs. Maude McGue	22 May 1925
John Marshall	Louetta Arington	17 May 1925
Max E. Poquette	Edith E. Hunt	23 May 1925
James L. Miller	Mrs. Ann Walker	23 May 1925
Roy Lewis	Helen Proctor	27 May 1925

GROOM	BRIDE	SOLEMNIZED
Chas. Gattis	Mrs. Linda Tallent	27 May1925
Luther Brown	Mrs. Lillie Moore	27 May 1925
Robert J. Kuper	Veronica M. Deken	27 May 1925
Alfred Lawson	Eula May Hulen	27 May 1925
Robert Smith	Lillian Dooley	28 May 1925
Herve Waddell	Zallie Ward	30 May 1925
W. P. Sutton	Mrs. Lena Yow	30 May 1925
Andrew Harding	Elsie Harper	31 May 1925
D. C. Morgan	Mrs. Willie Barnes	6 Jun 1925
H. F. Vaughn	Ida Garrison	8 Jun 1925
Henry Pruett	Birdie Burchett	5 Jun 1925
W. C. Rawson	Emma Smith	1 Jun 1925
A. M. Cheely	Grace Durham	31 May 1925
Vaughn Stigler	Maggie Range	11 Apr 1925
Chas. Neece	Flora Gobble	1 May 1925
W. E. Crocker	Lula W. Wilkerson	18 Apr 1925
Bernard Linnemann	Mrs. Petronella Bowles	21 Apr 1925
Geo. W. Connelly	Mrs. Della Ford	22 Apr 1925
Hubert G. Wilson	Essie Miller	18 Apr 1925
Loyd Monroe	Carrie Bohannon	5 Jun 1925
M. M. Hardwick	Mrs. Martha Bell Rogers	4 Jun 1925
Herman Wallis	Hattie Hearn	13 Jun 1925
J. M. Raspberry	Edna Davis	12 Jun 1925
Albert Abraham	Emma Statler	16 May 1925
Blackburn Night (Hight)	Francis Beck	3 Jun 1925
Julius Mitchell	Mattie Jackson	13 Jun 1925
M. P. Naylor	Mrs. Tevado Matlock	10 Jun 1925
David V. VanEckhoute	Henreitta Elma Doll	17 Jun 1925
Clell Estes	May Belle Eastridge	24 Jun 1925
E.J. Brockman	Rose Brockman	23 Jun 1925
O. L. Pippins	Etta Hallmark	21 Jun 1925
Elbert Nobles	Beulah Tate	20 Jun 1925
W. M. Hendrix	Rosa Ella Bell	19 Jun 1925
Cecil Fisher	Agnes Bilderback	27 Jun 1925
T. E. Slider	Neva Sloan	21 Jun 1925
Rollie Frazier	Dealie Stephens	25 Jun 1925
A. S. Ham	Olive Jane Aulsbury	25 Jun 1925
Claude Alexander Bounds	Pearl Vowell	1 Jul 1925
Joe Vinson	Alice Pitts	1 Mar 1925
Lenza Williams	Ruth Avery	14 Jun 1925
W. R. Rogers	Gertie Lacy	4 Jul 1925
Luther Davis	Lula Garrett	6 Jul 1925
Elmer Adams	Mrs. Beulah White	9 Jul 1925
Homer Eakins	Letha Faught	3 Jul 1925

GROOM	BRIDE	SOLEMNIZED
Jessie Jones	Stella Hobbs	11 Jul 1925
Herbert Thompson	Mrs. Lela Smith	13 Jul 1925
Salomon Jackson	Mrs. May Shaw	26 Jun 1925
Joe Whitehorn	Mrs. Tishie Pulley	4 Jul 1925
E. L. Householder	Mrs. Laurena Gruggett	18 Jul 1925
J. E. Call	M. B. Custer	12 Jul 1925
T. J. Jabbour	Afreeda Hamra	12 Jul 1925
Burl Bushong	Flosie Burcham	17 Jul 1925
T. S. Lane	Mary E. Green	Not Solemnized
C. P. Pittman	Nellie Redman	14 Jul 1925
Charlie Horner	Gertrude Radery	4 Jul 1925
Marvin Ridings	Florence Buck	10 Jul 1925
C. M. Frost	Mrs. Lela Delong	24 Jul 1925
William Boyd Mayes	Sarah Arebia Dean	26 Jul 1925
Leon Buttler	Magnolia Hix	20 Jul 1925
Orvil Oliver	Opal Sipes	25 Jul 1925
Chester Bone	Iva McIntosh	9 Jun 1925
R. J. Bishop	Clara Cook	26 Jul 1925
David Calder	Josie Creach	26 Jul 1925
Paul A. Slicer	Francis Brown	28 Jul 1925
Dolpherd Dees	Clara Hollis	31 Jul 1925
Eddie Caery	Mrs Annie Burks	31 Jul 1925
Ben Rushin	Nellie Duffy	1 Aug 1925
Greely Jaco	Odessie Combs	18 Jul 1925
A. W. Torrence	Jewell Melton	3 Aug 1925
E. L. Williams	Annie Palmer	5 Aug 1925
John Odum	Mrs. Gertie Horner	24 Jul 1925
Arthur J. Erwin	Thelma Francis Singleton	5 Aug 1925
James Qualls	Gertrude Gobble	5 Aug 1925
Len Nels	Mabel Huff	5 Aug 1925
Ewell White	Bell Psalmands	6 Aug 1925
Burley Trantham	Lee Fleeman	7 Aug 1925
Nort Thornberry	Myrtle Masterson	8 Aug 1925
Ray Lowery	Marce Phillips	8 Aug 1925
Walter K. Busby	Ruth Dougherty	8 Aug 1925
Paul Lewis	Violet Sykes	10 Aug 1925
Albert Johnson	Bertha Westbrook	6 Jul 1925
Tom Holifield	Verna Cole	12 Aug 1925
Ashly Draper	Myrtle Powers	17 Aug 1925
William L. Holbrook	Lucy Herrell	17 Aug 1925
Curtis Burchett	May Knight	19 Aug 1925
James McCrystal	Amey Wickman	18 Aug 1925
Oscar Miller	Ollie Lenard	26 Aug 1925
Jessie Whitley	Ella Hildebrand	9 Aug 1925

GROOM	BRIDE	SOLEMNIZED
Clarence Ward	Ellen Hearn	15 Aug 1925
Fred M. Boring	Bessie R. Hartwell	23 Aug 1925
Archie Cook	Mrs. Mary Clark	14 Jul 1925
Ben Jarrett	Florine Phillips	22 Aug 1925
Arthur Williams	Willie Wallace	25 Aug 1925
J. H. Chandler	Lillie Chamberlain	25 Aug 1925
W. H. Mulherin	Mrs. Verna Love	25 Aug 1925
Willie L. Lewis	Mrs. Vera McCulley	27 Aug 1925
Johnie Thompson	Iva Blocker	29 Aug 1925
William Carman	Nellie Rutledge	28 Aug 1925
Roy Richard Benfield	Ethel Morgan	29 Aug 1925
John Huey	Maude Collins	23 Aug 1925
Hughie McNail	Pearl Griffin	31 Aug 1925
Charlie Maulden	Amanda Masterson	1 Sep 1925
Jim Fletcher	Maudie J. Cole	3 Sep 1925
T. C. Rauls	Mrs. Beulah Hendrix	25 Jun 1925
Shannon B. Pool	Velma E. Coughlin	26 Jul 1925
Elmer Ray	Dora Bohannon	18 Aug 1925
John Abbott	Edith Green	4 Sep 1925
Sam Gifford	Pearl Montgomery	5 Sep 1925
William Lowe	Thelma Read	3 Sep 1925
Joe Hall	Myrtle Cook	4 Sep 1925
O. J. Vance	Josie Bunch	6 Sep 1925
Ralph Carr	Rena Gibson	7 Sep 1925
Fred Mason	Ethel Ryan	5 Sep 1925
John Hitt	Mary Fowler	9 Sep 1925
J. H. Pettiejohn	Georg Alice Craig	11 Sep 1925
J. L. Hodges	Mrs. Emma Bartley	14 Sep 1925
Johnnie Burk (Buck)	Nellie Redman	12 Sep 1925
James Gentry	Lora Harvey	8 Sep 1925
R. D. Moore	Mrs. Minnie Chilton	13 Sep 1925
Harvey Tinnin	Lizzie Parrysh	13 Sep 1925
William Busby	Ruth Biggs	12 Sep 1925
Clarence Hurt	Ethel Bowman	15 Sep 1925
James E. Brown	Willie Pearl Pool	16 Sep 1925
T. M. Ladyman	Hattie Keer	19 Sep 1925
Estel Newson	Ina Mae Daily	20 Sep 1925
William Thomas Sawyer	Audrey Byrd	22 Sep 1925
Clarence Combs	Bessie Bullie	22 Sep 1925
J. M. McClure	Mrs. Lizzie Carmichael	23 Sep 1925
M. V. Beck	Belle Copeland	23 Sep 1925
Dan Atnips	Dollie Sinks	21 Sep 1925
L. Hampton	Mrs. Gertrude Fowler	22 Sep 1925
Bennie Clark	Pearl Schaffer	26 Sep 1925

GROOM	BRIDE	SOLEMNIZED
Price Ham	Janet Waddell	27 Sep 1925
Alton Cousins	Virgie Barton	24 Sep 1925
Tim Garner	Minnie Finley	26 Sep 1925
Ruben Bailey	Anna Bell Whittaker	26 Sep 1925
William Bess	Rutha Barred	26 Sep 1925
Ray Pierson	Vera Barringer	1 Oct 1925
Wiley N. Smith	Beulah McCormick	2 Oct 1925
Robert Marshall	Bessie Chailland	1 Oct 1925
Carlile Thompson	Lizzie McDole	2 Oct 1925
Thos. Frans	Estelle Kilgore	3 Oct 1925
Johny Goodwin	Lettie Irne Long	3 Oct 1925
Louis Watson	Mary Williams	4 Oct 1925
Barney Hendryx	Gertie Elder	5 Oct 1925
Nute Abney	Gladys Carr	6 Oct 1925
Robert C. Clark	Gladys Pauline Caldwell	13 Aug 1925
Jessie F. Patterson	Pauline V. Blankenship	7 Oct 1925
J. W. Woodard	Annie Davis	8 Oct 1925
Doss Smithwick	Bessie Low	8 Oct 1925
David P. Watson	Minnie Walker	9 Oct 1925
Lema Thompson	Bertha Jackson	9 Oct 1925
George Taylor	Goldie Horner	10 Oct 1925
Earl Harris	Myrtle Edwards	10 Oct 1925
B. C. Patterson	Ethel Breedlove	11 Oct 1925
Harvey Collins	Addie Mitchell	10 Oct 1925
James Henry Robeson	Mabel Myrtle Meyer	13 Oct 1925
W. G. Harris	Mrs. Allie B. Brazier	5 Sep 1925
Ed Whitaker	Beulah McClish	1 Oct 1925
Allie Horner	Dorsie Brown	3 Oct 1925
Leslie Parker	Lillie Kaiser	16 Oct 1925
Henry Kuper	Grace E. Freedman	15 Oct 1925
Loy Lancaster	Maudie Grimsley	10 Oct 1925
Henry Miller	Hettie Davis	10 Sep 1925
Burl Milbourn	Louise Liggett	3 Oct 1925
Claud Goodman	Thelma Williams	17 Oct 1925
Waren Stirling Akins	Ora Coleman	1 Sep 1925
Charley Greer	Elva Rhodes	17 Oct 1925
M. E. Wilson	Edna McDonald	17 Oct 1925
Frankie Smullin	Vadie Barringer	18 Oct 1925
Timothy McClanahan	Ila Williams	18 Oct 1925
Fred Brown	Laura Snider	19 Oct 1925
Jim Clark	Liza Graves	3 Oct 1925
J. T. Denison	Dotta May Bolin	17 Oct 1925
J. G. Watson	Birtrice Wells	24 Oct 1925
Wallis Norris	Lola Pirdly	7 Oct 1925

GROOM	BRIDE	SOLEMNIZED
W. B. Revel	Martha Stewart	26 Oct 1925
T. J. Collins	Mary L. Dye	23 Oct 1925
Wesley Griffith	Della Belle Osborn	23 Oct 1925
Dee Hitt	Birdie Randl	17 Oct 1925
Charley Mitchner	Ada Shaw	4 Oct 1925
Jimmie Morris	Alice Laird	28 Oct 1925
Phillip W. Rennell	Anna Willard	28 Oct 1925
Oliver Boshers	Mora White	28 Oct 1925
William Fred Stratman	Cecillia Fortman	28 Oct 1925
Fred Harmon	Gladys Linhart	31 Oct 1925
Everett Osburn	Nola Johnson	27 Oct 1925
F. M. Williams	Mary Jones	31 Oct 1925
Clarence Masterson	Hattie Dublin	25 Oct 1925
Nelson Parnell	Zola Thorn	1 Nov 1925
Frank Bryant	Genevieve Rhyne	2 Nov 1925
W. L. Whitehead	Mandy L. Bratcher	3 Nov 1925
W. O. Hodge	Lillie Bailey Farmer	3 Nov 1925
George Walton	Freeda Burchett	4 Nov 1925
Elmer James Langdon	Lena Beatrice Minetree	5 Nov 1925
Henry Emery	Bernize Harmon	5 Nov 1925
Sam Johson (Johnson)	Liza Lee	8 Nov 1925
Joe Long	Delia Barnett	7 Nov 1925
Virgil J. Smith	Pearl Eakers	7 Nov 1925
Clarence E. Gulley	Bernice Moore	8 Nov 1925
Edward Hinkle	Ruth Prance	9 Nov 1925
Willie E. Marshall	Lela Robertson	8 Nov 1925
Shelton Williamson	Pearl Bramlett	7 Nov 1925
Elmer Williams	Gertie Thornton	10 Nov 1925
Thurston Smith	Mildred Frost	12 Nov 1925
Edgar Boyd	Anna Lane	18 Oct 1925
Robert Sparks	Myrtle Johnson	4 Sep 1925
John Watson	Ruth Lasley	12 Nov 1925
Willie Laird	Lillie May	14 Nov 1925
Obine Wyatt	Okla Henderson	14 Nov 1925
V. K. McGrew	Kate Abney	14 Nov 1925
Dick Smith	Mrs. Nettie Revelle	14 Nov 1925
Lloyd Curtis	Fredie Wilson	15 Nov 1925
Sam Mikel	Mrs. Nora Jones Campbell	12 Nov 1925
Marshal Earp	Mary Pitts	14 Nov 1925
J. W. Pile	Florence Whittaker	14 Nov 1925
Albert Branch	Malinda Lane	19 Nov 1925
J. W. Ratliff	Opal Lucile Woods	15 Nov 1925
Burk Mosley	Beatrice Smith	16 Nov 1925
Raymond Maples	Alice Wortham	17 Nov 1925

GROOM	BRIDE	SOLEMNIZED
Wm. E. Cox	Mrs. S. M. Oakley	21 Nov 1925
Joe Williams	Lucy Scott	21 Nov 1925
Dewer Joyner	Icey Mitchell	21 Nov 1925
Jim Canady	Bessie Snider	21 Nov 1925
Burley Gothard	Genera Gray	22 Nov 1925
Charley Johnson	Pricillia Howard	14 Nov 1925
Harry Van Wagner	Annie Cook	25 Nov 1925
Herman J. Finder	Cicero Rummage	25 Nov 1925
Johnny Hamilton	Myrtle Hanners	28 Nov 1925
Tharwell V. Taylor	Opal Fortner	29 Nov 1925
Frank W Casteel	Jewel Lewis	26 Nov 1925
Claud Hodges	Nellie Haislip	22 Nov 1925
Marion Sullivan	MyrtleAustin	28 Nov 1925
Frank Westmoreland	Altha Pattillo	16 Nov 1925
George Edward Armstrong	Sallie Taber	1 Dec 1925
Asa L. White	Helen C. Caneer	22 Nov 1925
James Williams	Patsey Varner	2 Dec 1925
Andy Sissom	Elsie Cross	3 Dec 1925
Clarence Gray	Lottie Middleton	28 Nov 1925
Robert Pruett	Opal Riddle	9 Dec 1925
Emmett King	Lossie Wise	5 Dec 1925
Johnny Owens	Pearley May Lacy	10 Dec 1925
Marion Cooper	Ollie Cowell	5 Dec 1925
John L. Ray	Ethel Randal	9 Dec 1925
J. William Smith	Lidey Hataway	10 Dec 1925
Claud J. Hunt	Sadie Bramlett	12 Dec 1925

Abbott, 108, 113
Abernathy, 97
Abney, 114-115
Abraham, 111
Aburshan, 109
Adams, 96, 100, 103, 111
Adkins, 100, 106
Adolph, 103
Akers, 96
Akins, 114
Akridge, 110
Albertson, 106
Albright, 99
Alford, 102
Allen, 97-98, 105
Anders, 96
Anderson, 105-106, 110
Andrews, 110
Annis, 95
Anniston, 95
Arington, 110
Armour, 98
Armstrong, 116
Arnold, 95-96
Atchley, 99
Atnips, 113
Auction, 105
Aulsbury, 111
Austin, 99, 102, 104, 116
Avery, 111
Ayres, 98, 106
Bachelor, 100
Bailey, 96, 108, 114
Baird, 95
Baker, 95-97, 99-100
Baldridge, 104
Baldwin, 102
Ball, 100
Bankston, 100, 108

Banthrall, 107
Barber, 97, 100, 110,
Barger, 104
Barham, 100-101
Barnes, 96-97, 105-106, 111
Barnett, 95, 115
Barred, 114
Barringer, 114
Bartley, 113
Barton, 97, 114
Bassinger, 106-107
Batchelor, 103
Battles, 105
Baum, 100
Bayles, 96
Bean, 108
Beardsley, 108
Beck, 111, 113
Becker, 106
Beeman, 98
Bell, 111
Benfield, 113
Benline, 107
Benton, 109
Berline, 107
Berry, 97, 103, 107
Bess, 100, 114
Bester, 110
Bethel, 99
Biggs, 102, 106, 110, 113
Bilderback, 111
Binkley, 101
Birchfield, 102
Bishop, 97
Blakemore, 97, 100, 107,
Blanchard, 101, 109
Blankenship, 98, 105, 114
Blaze, 105

Bledsoe, 102
Blevings, 105
Blocker, 113
Blount, 108
Boatwright, 100
Bohannon, 101, 108, 111, 113
Bolin, 114
Bonaby, 110
Bone, 112
Boring, 113
Boshers, 115
Bounds, 111
Bounds, 98
Bowles, 104, 111
Bowman, 102, 113
Boyd, 107, 115
Boyer, 110
Braden, 101, 108
Bradford, 97
Bramlett, 115-116
Branch, 104, 106, 115
Brannon, 95, 102
Brannum, 96
Bratcher, 115
Brazier, 114
Breedlove, 114
Bridges, 110
Briggs, 103
Britt, 107
Brockman, 111
Bronson, 100
Brooks, 103
Brown, 95-97, 100-101, 103-104, 108-109, 111-114
Brunt, 109
Bryant, 102, 115
Buck, 109, 112-113
Bullie, 113
Bullins, 107
Bunch, 113

Holder, 98
Holifield, 98, 101, 112
Hollis, 112
Holly, 96
Holmes, 103, 107
Holt, 102
Honeycut, 103
Hopkins, 102
Hopper, 96
Hopson, 97
Hopwood, 98
Hormer, 110
Horner, 98, 110, 112, 114
Horseman, 103
Houchins, 105
Householder, 112
Housen, 95
Howard, 96, 102, 109, 116
Howe, 103
Hubbard, 98, 103
Hubbell, 103
Hudgins, 101
Huey, 113
Huff, 112
Huffman, 109
Hughes, 96, 103, 110
Hulen, 99, 111
Hull, 108
Hunt, 110, 116
Hurst, 107
Hurston, 103
Hurt, 104, 113
Husketh, 106
Huston, 95
Hutchinson, 103
Insco, 104
Irvin, 109
Isbell, 104
Ivy, 101
Jabbour, 112
Jackson, 95, 99, 102, 105-106, 111-112, 114

Jaco, 112
James, 97-98, 101-102, 104, 108
Jarrett, 113
Jarvis, 108
Jeffords, 101
Jenkins, 106
Jennings, 109
Johnson, 95-97, 100, 102, 105-108, 110, 112, 115-116
Johson, 115
Joiner, 101
Jolly, 101
Jones, 96, 98, 102-103, 105-106, 108-109, 112, 115
Jordan, 98
Jordon, 104
Joyner, 100
Joyner, 116
Julian, 98, 106
Justice, 98
Kaiser, 114
Kean, 96
Keaton, 100
Keeer, 113
Keen, 102
Keith, 101
Kelley, 96, 107
Kelly, 98
Kennon, 98
Kent, 99
Key, 98
Keys, 99
Kibler, 104
Kilgore, 114
Killbreth, 100
Killian, 98, 109
Kimbrow, 99
Kime, 97
Kinchen, 102
Kinder, 97
King, 95, 99, 116
Kinser, 106
Kinsolving, 96

Kinzey, 108
Kirby, 104, 109
Kirkman, 97, 99
Kitchell, 101
Knight, 112
Knox, 102
Kuper, 111, 114
Kyle, 97
Laber, 95
Lacy, 106, 109, 111, 116
Ladyman, 113
Lafont, 95
Laird, 115
Lambert, 103
Lamunion, 98
Lancaster, 99, 114
Landers, 108
Landreth, 95, 98
Landrum, 97, 105
Lane, 101, 107, 112, 115
Langdon, 115
Langford, 104
Langley, 108-109
Lanier, 106
Lasley, 115
Lasswell, 99
Lawson, 111
Layton, 101
Leatherman, 102
Lebo, 101
Ledbetter, 109
Lee, 99, 102-103, 108, 115
Leggon, 104
Legon, 103
Lemonds, 107
Lenard, 112
Lester, 107
Lewis, 102-103, 108-110, 112-113, 116
Liggett, 114
Lillard, 95
Lincoln, 103
Lines, 96

Volume 16A December to October 1921

Though there are very few records for colored marriages in Dunklin County, the use of col for colored does show up a few times.

GROOM	BRIDE	SOLEMNIZED
Burnell Banthrall	Cora E. Drew	6 Dec 1921
Curtis Walker	Mrs. Amy Jones	4 Dec 1921
Bill Ragsdale	Monnie Bohannon	3 Dec 1921
Sidney Felker	Dannie Harman	4 Dec 1921
Luther M. Hinshaw	Ruby Halsey	4 Dec 1921
R. W. Biggs	M. E. Brazell	24 Nov 1921
N. H. Needham	Dollie Allen	3 Dec 1921
C. M. Evans	Ethel Kirk	26 Nov 1921
I. C. Provo	Lela York	27 Nov 1921
Wain Rickman	Lula Mabrye	26 Nov 1921
Floyd Richard Darby	Vadia Harper	23 Nov 1921
W. J. Hobbs	Maggie Young	22 Nov 1921
Otto Gross	Reavealter Thomas	20 Nov 1921
Jim Ruddick	Ethel Hubbard	22 Nov 1921
Larkin M. Moneyham	Mrs. Anna Dent	21 Nov 1921
Zona Holloway	Ora Bell Davis	20 Nov 1921
Joseph I. Knott	Marguerite C. Clancy	23 Nov 1921
Hardy Pleasant Billington	Opal Lee Shipman	19 Nov 1921
Sylvester Johnson	Lillian Stacy	19 Nov 1921
Robert Hasking Parrish	Laura Jane Arndell	20 Nov 1921
N. M. Ford	Allene Brown	11 Nov 1921
Chas. J. Lewis	Edith Lewis	10 Nov 1921
J. W. McCallam	Immer Terry	6 Nov 1921
Chas. Q. Moore Jr.	Vera Noland	6 Nov 1921
Wilburn Fish	Lottie Johnson	6 Nov 1921
Clarence Powell	Alta Davis	5 Nov 1921
Robert Brotherton	Pearl Kirby	6 Nov 1921
Paul A. Redmond	Katherine White	9 Nov 1921
Geo. W. Harris	Edith Gune	2 Nov 1921
Tommie Owen	Bessie Johnson	23 Oct 1921
Chas. F. Miller	Andie (Audie) Wilkinson	22 Oct 1921
W. T. Alexander	Mrs. Alice Easley	5 Oct 1921

Alexander, 127
Allen, 127
Banthrall, 127
Biggs, 127
Billington, 127
Bohannon, 127
Brazell, 127
Brotherton, 127
Brown, 127
Clancy, 127
Darby, 127
Davis, 127
Dent, 127
Drew, 127
Easley, 127
Evans, 127
Felker, 127
Fish, 127
Ford, 127
Gross, 127

Gune, 127
Halsey, 127
Harman, 127
Harper, 127
Harris, 127
Hirshaw, 127
Hobbs, 127
Holloway, 127
Hubbard, 127
Johnson, 127
Jones, 127
Kirby, 127
Kirk, 127
Knott, 127
Lewis, 127
Mabrye, 127
McCallam, 127
Miller, 127
Moneyham, 127
Moore, 127

Neeham, 127
Noland, 127
Owen, 127
Powell, 127
Provo, 127
Ragsdale, 127
Redmon, 127
Redmond, 127
Rickman, 127
Ruddick, 127
Shipman, 127
Stacy, 127
Terry, 127
Thomas, 127
Walker, 127
White, 127
Wilkinson, 127
York, 127
Young, 127

Volume 17 1925-1927

Though there are very few records for colored marriages in Dunklin County, the use of col for colored does show up a few times. There is one 1924 date.

GROOM	BRIDE	SOLEMNIZED
Ira Dosser	Mrs. Cora Neely	12 Dec 1925
Peat Pope	Rena Crafton	14 Dec 1925
Noah Blount	Edith Hodges	28 Nov 1925
Elgen Neely	Virgie Lentz	22 Dec 1925
Walter Harris	Mary Anne Jones	27 Aug 1925
E. P. Meyers	Ollie M. Worley	21 Dec 1925
Guy Bartley	Ethel Moore	28 Nov 1925
T. H. Raimges	Lula Brown	18 Dec 1925
M. H. Bazzell	Mrs. Lizzie McKabee	19 Dec 1925
John L. Bostic	Jeanett Arends	17 Dec 1925
David Kincannon	Martha Greenway	11 Oct 1925
Charles A. Sheets	Mrs. Laura Hurt	16 Dec 1925
Norman Harbison	Eva Hutchison	23 Dec 1925
M. J. Tillman	Mandy Scarbrough	19 Nov 1925
Lilburn Turner	Lois Buckley	22 Dec 1925
George Daves	Mrs. Mary Williams	19 Dec 1925
C. V. Walkins	Rachel Barrett	24 Dec 1925
Jake McClain	Cermilla Moris	24 Dec 1925
Henry Ward	Velma Redding	24 Dec 1925
Joseph C. James	May Blades	24 Dec 1925
Robert Bunch	Elma Sherrill	15 Dec 1925
Earl Barnes	Ruth Oliver	23 Dec 1925
J. T. Maness	Goldie Mae Alsup	21 Dec 1925
Lester Phelps	Dora Burnes	25 Dec 1925
J. F. Rushing	Mrs. Alice Louise Reves	25 Dec 1925
S. A. Fletcher Govan	Lillie Wilson	29 Dec 1925
Clayton Haycraft	Aleen Gibson	24 Dec 1925
J. C. Mills	Helen Randol	29 Dec 1925
Oscar Peddago	Hilla Goodman	25 Dec 1925
C. M. Leach	Mrs. Mary Leach	31 Dec 1925
Verden Johnson	Nora Jarrett	1 Jan 1926
Lester Reis	Ethel Baker	31 Dec 1925
Irl R. Richardson	Pearl B. Snider	28 Dec 1925
J. C. Brittain	Anna Dartt	30 Dec 1925
H. T. Castole	Mrs. Minnie Thorp	24 Dec 1925

GROOM	BRIDE	SOLEMNIZED
C. K. Bryant	Maddie Gregory	26 Dec 1925
Harry L. Howllett	Candras Troxler	4 Jan 1926
John Stigler	Nellie Patterson	22 Dec 1925
Lawrence Lauben (Lauten)	Ola Halegan	1 Jan 1926
J. A. Gordon	Queenie Ray	5 Jan 1926
Palmer Johnson	Gertrude Loyd	6 Jan 1926
Floyd Ralph Taylor	Beatrice McCombs	14 Jan 1926
Harry Prince	Pearl Johnson	14 Jan 1926
William Lewis	Mrs. Charlotte Woodard	8 Jan 1926
Albert Williams	Pearl White	11 Jan 1926
Louis Hickerson	Agness Grogan	10 Jan 1926
Rush C. Smith	Octa A. Bennett	8 Jan 1926
Buron Simmons	Maude Sitz	11 Jan 1926
Ray J. Belt	Myrtle Morris	9 Jan 1926
E. N. Catton	L. E. Womack	16 Jan 1926
Hollis Tendal	Mabel Wright	16 Jan 1926
T. D. Davis	Odie Knight	17 Jan 1926
Joe Ellwood	Ethyle Goodwin	18 Jan 1926
Edward Underhill	Ethel Eastridge	20 Jan 1926
Earl Knight	Bessie Thompson	12 Jan 1926
W. H. Thornton	Lillie McKenzie	19 Jan 1926
Charley Gum	Ruth Myrl Green	21 Jan 1926
W. R. Morris	Mrs. Eva Sanders	22 Jan 1926
Robert Blackburn	Lula Bowman	16 Jan 1926
C. R. Branum	Velma Davis	25 Jan 1926
O. A. Williams	Mrs. Mina Hardin	24 Jan 1926
Frank F. Dudley	Helen Poe	28 Jan 1926
A. B. Thomas	Alcie Bell Miller	28 Dec 1925
Zannier Wood	Geneve Lancaster	28 Jan 1926
Paul Eberhart	Gertrude Wiseman	1 Feb 1926
J. L. Grooms	May Cannon	1 Feb 1926
Coy Batton	Cherry Turpin	31 Jan 1926
Sidney House	Mattie Shepard	31 Jan 1926
Edward A. Douglass	Jennie D. Woods	31 Jan 1926
Claud Riley	Acey Harrison	11 Feb 1926
Charles Willard	Lois Mitchell	6 Jan 1926
Vernon Ray	Avis Tucker	8 Feb 1926
W. H. Hutchins	Mollie Wallace	3 Feb 1926
T. S. Houchins	Meade Sisco	8 Feb 1926
Y. T. Atson	Blanch Stigler	6 Feb 1926
Eugene Williams	Ora Lee Greer (Green)	6 Feb 1926
Joe Masterson	Dora Jones	10 Feb 1926
W. E. Chitman	Rhoda M. Lell	9 Feb 1926
Rosewell Bennett	Mattie Jackson	5 Feb 1926

GROOM	BRIDE	SOLEMNIZED
William McPherson	Lillie M. Valintine	9 Feb 1926
Roy Jorden	Opal Cook	6 Feb 1926
William Bolin	Maggie Hurt	30 Jan 1926
Sam Mizell	Myrtle Mizell	6 Feb 1926
B. W. Westmoreland	Mrs. Sarah Casey	7 Feb 1926
J. W. Murray	Nora Edgin	11 Feb 1926
Read Belt	Gladys Scarlet	4 Feb 1926
Lee Scarlet	Christine McGahey	13 Feb 1926
Charley Anderson	Lucy Gilliam	30 Jan 1926
W. F. Lamunion	Iza Izoia Landers	10 Feb 1926
Jimmie Gabbard	Stell May Moore	24 Feb 1926
Homer Arnold	Charity Gaines	20 Feb 1926
M. Black	Verda Kennedy	21 Feb 1926
R. L. Berkley	Ada Davis	17 Feb 1926
Paul E. Liggett	Kathlees Perry	13 Jan 1926
Ogle Bishop	Hazel Malone	23 Feb 1926
Lee Steele	Myrtle Elder	27 Feb 1926
Boner Zook	Myrtle Sinclair	23 Feb 1926
H. E. Roach	Lizzie Chumley	1 Mar 1926
A. W. Bratcher	Marion Byrd Minton	27 Feb 1926
W. Marvin Haire	Blanche H. Merrick	27 Feb 1926
Jeff Marvin Hawkins	Cresa Phillips	17 Jan 1926
Charles Fleemond	Ortha Anderson	27 Feb 1926
F. W. Hall	Anthby Erwin	12 Mar 1926
Oscar Bailey	Myrtle Bunting	6 Mar 1926
Hartford Williams	Florence Zimmerman	12 Mar 1926
T. C. Salter	Erley(Erby) Holton	13 Mar 1926
James Weaver	Mrs. Grace McCarty	14 Mar 1926
Elmer Henley	Agness Nuckolls	11 Mar 1926
Manley Horner	Ethel Rhew	20 Mar 1926
Lindell Johnson	Mildred D. Pike	19 Mar 1926
Arther Holliday	Nettie B. Stevenson	20 Mar 1926
Roy Fisher	Ella Blackman	14 Mar 1926
Fred Dohrman	Mrs. Della Henry	25 Mar 1926
Audley (Andley) V. Smith	Eldridge Karlish	30 Jan 1926
Truman Ponder	Beulah Milburn	27 Mar 1926
John A. Stewart	Katie Smith	29 Mar 1926
John Rudder	Audra Beauchamp	27 Mar 1926
Arthur M. Crim	Mrs. Flora Heath	5 Apr 1926
Jessie Mayberry	Helen Lewis	5 Apr 1926
Connard Brown	Bessie Wills	7 Apr 1926
Richard Cato	Esther Hart	3 Apr 1926
J. W. Davis	Bonnie Barnes	8 Apr 1926
Frank Pervitt	Lizzie Pervitt	10 Mar 1926

GROOM	BRIDE	SOLEMNIZED
John Brewer (col)	Louisa Clark (col)	11 Apr 1926
David Firmbanks	Alene Jones	10 Apr 1926
Scott Murphy	Lola Nolen	10 Apr 1926
William Thompson	Lieuinda Gordon	13 Apr 1926
J. H. Jones	Perdelia T. Lutes	17 Apr 1926
Julius Barrett	Ester Watkins	17 Apr 1926
Ralph Olds	Opal Standridge	17 Apr 1926
John Jones	Fannie Thompson	18 Apr 1926
Henry Garland	Elza Brooks	26 Apr 1926
Louis Dortch	Lola Smith	22 Mar 1926
Everett Allen	Opal Avery	24 Feb 1926
John Alsup	Lula Hart	24 Apr 1926
Aubrey Crow	Daisy Boker (Baker)	26 Apr 1926
Wiley Luallen	Johnie B. Mills	24 Apr 1926
Robert King	Annie Frank	3 May 1926
Thomas E. Wyatt	Velma Anderson	30 Apr 1926
Joe Eason	Mrs. Nellie McRoy	28 Apr 1926
J. C. Smith	Mrs. Sarah Harmon	1 May 1926
Brule O'Dell	Mrs. Ima Grimes	2 May 1926
T. K. Williams	Eva Mae Buchanan	3 May 1926
John Morris	Ella Triplett	8 May 1926
H. Garner	Ghissell Hall	8 May 1926
E. O. Masters	Dovie Ford	8 May 1926
William Drew	Lena Benthrall	8 May 1926
S. J. Sparks	Ruth Jones	11 May 1926
J. H. Welty	Bernice Hanks	9 May 1926
C. L. Culp	Alta May Gary	24 Apr 1926
James Hardin	Mrs. Rosa Allen	12 May 1926
W. J. Thomas	Fay Brydon	12 May 1926
Claud Sullivan	Jessie Barton	13 May 1926
Wm. Arthur Reed	Nina Burns	15 May 1926
Ernest L. Marshall	Lillian Englehardt	14 May 1926
S. M. Broughs	Mrs. Rosy Story	15 Mar 1926
Otto Bell	Emma Ernest	10 Apr 1926
A. E. Browers	Ola May Browers	13 May 1926
Paul Wilson	May Cooper	31 May 1926
J. E. Carter	Irene Carter	17 May 1926
T. H. Dye	Etta E. Grogan	15 May 1926
Joe Boyd	Eva Pounds	2 May 1926
L. T. Brown	Mrs. Sarah Ann Redden	2 May 1926
Charley Hart	Lucy Hart	4 May 1926
Doyle Lackey	Mildred Green	17 May 1926
Willic Estcst	Mrs. Carric Pendleton	15 May 1926
Willis Renfroe	Luvicie Robertson	22 May 1926

GROOM	BRIDE	SOLEMNIZED
O. R. Martin	Pearl Golden	13 May 1926
Howard Miller	Irene Griffin	21 May 1926
C. R. Lemonds	Mrs. Myrtle Jarvis	22 May 1926
T. L. Young	Lena Hawkins	22 May 1926
Elza Tarno (Tarvo)	Larine Key	22 May 1926
B. S. Eskew	Maty Shields	25 May 1926
J. C. Cardell	Gertrenee Burkell	29 May 1926
Noah White	Mary Smith	31 May 1926
W. Williamson	Mrs. Ella Parish	30 May 1926
J. H. Williams	Lyle Vardell	1 Jun 1926
J. F. Mullikin	Alewe M. Petty	4 Apr 1926
Andrew Johnson	Mrs. Florence Harden	29 May 1926
P. G. Hughes	Mrs. John Parker	3 Jun 1926
J. C. Dobbs	Marie Mewson	26 May 1926
Robert E. Snodgrass	Frances Ferguson	29 May 1926
Thelmer Thomas	Irene Johnson	6 Jun 1926
Russsell (Rusom)Davis	Thelma Oakes	14 Jun 1926
Ralph E. Broderick	Hermena Anthony	15 Jun 1926
A. C. Clayton	Jewell Gray	Not Solemnized
Lenard Patrick	Retha Malone	20 Jun 1926
Eugene M. Taylor	Eula Maxine Lanier	21 Jun 1926
Jim Johnson	Mrs. Add Meely	18 Jun 1926
August Skinner	May Skinner (Dense)	23 Jun 1926
William E. Brewer	Maud Williams	19 Jun 1926
R. M. Ownby	Savannah Kimbrow	24 Jun 1926
Tommy Riley	Mrs. Minnie Atnip	29 Jun 1926
Wm. Whitfield	Mrs. Rose Tucker	18 May 1926
Ray Mc Callum	Zora Montgomery	Not Solemized
Steve Clayton	Alberta Williams	13 Jun 1926
Chas. Berry	Mrs. Lizzie Wilson	27 Jun 1926
Loyd James	Luciel Lovelace	24 Apr 1926
Dan Wyatt	Ardis Maylene Rowland	13 Jan 1926
B. B. Phillips	Lillie M. Ray	3 Jul 1926
Marcus Derryberry	Vera Cary	4 Jul 1926
Fred Wallace	Veda Wilson	4 Jul 1926
Herman Runyon	Beulah Capper	5 Jul 1926
Charles E. Benton	Mrs. Fannie Miller	Not Solemnized
T. S. Smith	Mara Herman	19 Jun 1926
Hue Canaday	Otis Brown	26 Jun 1926
Fred Ackley	Glenda Pruett	3 Jul 1926
Tarrie Melton	Mary Jane Houchins	10 Jul 1926
Fred Golden	Lula Houchins	12 Jul 1926
W. H. Peterson	Hester Lucile Shaver	11 Jul 1926
W. J. Purvis	Minnie Tackeberry	13 Jul 1926

GROOM	BRIDE	SOLEMNIZED
Robert Lee Weeks	Mrs. Kate Burk	10 Jul 1926
Mannie Merideth	Elizabeth Eastridge	12 Jul 1926
Ben Ferguson	Eilene Ferguson	16 Jul 1926
H. B. Parker	Mrs. M. G. Braden	11 Jul 1926
J. M. Godby	Mrs. Ella Blackwell	17 Jul 1926
Elliott Jennings	Mayme Winchester	17 Jul 1926
Loren Smith	Mrs. Viola Fulgum	13 Jul 1926
Austin F. Winchester	Susan Anvil Morris	18 Jul 1926
C. H. McMurphy	Lila D. Wilson	26 Jul 1926
Robert Smith	Katherine Arendell	21 Jul 1926
George Street	Lola Minor	21 Jul 1926
John McLean	Mrs. Sarah Campbell	24 Jul 1926
C. W. Patterson	Mary Johnson	25 Jul 1926
Louis Thompson	Lela Alluran	28 Jul 1926
Ray Hul	Ruby Jenkins	28 Jul 1926
James Vincent	Lillian Taylor	24 Jul 1926
A. E. Phillips	Ruby Combs	30 Jul 1926
Louis Smith	Pearl White	2 Aug 1926
Ronald D. Ward	Lottie M. Lanier	31 Jul 1926
S. R. Whiteau	Edith Morris	3 Aug 1926
E. E. Anderson	Lucile Kinnamon	7 Aug 1926
C. R. Douhitt	Alice Wynn	7 Aug 1926
Glenn Johnson	Drucile Hinton	10 Aug 1926
James L. Hancock	Clyde Portensad	27 Jul 1926
Alfred McCormick	Myrtle Wallace	14 Aug 1926
Seldon Pillow	Gertrude Jackson	13 Aug 1926
J. T. Ward	Mrs. Pearl Harris	16 Aug 1926
Clyde Hudgens	Mattie Doak	17 Aug 1926
J. W. Alexander Jr.	Mary Kohlwick	19 Aug 1926
Howard Clifton McLain	Nettie May Neill	21 Aug 1926
Otto Fields	Maudie Johnson	1 Aug 1926
J. M. Blackman	Mrs. Dena Harvill	21 Aug 1926
S. K. Aspray	Mrs. Stella Brown	21 Aug 1926
R. M. Jackson	Mrs. Josephine Hinkles	22 Aug 1926
Paul S. Beasley	May Elsie Williams	26 Aug 1926
Tom Coleman	Mrs. Irene Griggs	25 Aug 1926
Joe Coupples	Clara Prince	21 Aug 1926
Reno Bailey	Dutie (Deetie) McCullough	25 Aug 1926
G. W. Cross	Iva Cross	28 Aug 1926
Roy Oliver	Dora E. Parish	28 Aug 1926
Calvin York	Irma Walker	26 Aug 1926
Sam Allison	Lucy Slemky	16 Aug 1926
William Gore	Elen Carter	3 Sep 1926
Jim Barfield	Rosa Davis	6 Sep 1926

GROOM	BRIDE	SOLEMNIZED
Frank R. Mapel	Virginia E. Pollock	6 Sep 1926
Henry Bailey	Ella Pitts	8 Sep 1926
John Polys	Charlesetta Mattingly	8 Sep 1926
R. E. Cole	Mrs. Ruth Stone	17 Sep 1926
Cecil Sickler	Mrs. Rachel Cullens Oldham	10 Sep 1926
Paul Carey	Catherine Mobley	28 Sep 1926
H. P. Dean	Olene Stone	11 Sep 1926
John Lawson	Ellen Meadows	11 Sep 1926
Jonas Allen	Juanita Medling	7 Sep 1926
A. A. Davault	Norma Allison	11 Sep 1926
W. V. Thomas	Verdie Johnson	12 Sep 1926
William Luker	Mrs. Mary Fike	11 Sep 1926
Majer Wm. Ray	Mabel E. Williams	15 Aug 1926
Huey Sifford	Lula Hicklin	Not Solemnized
Bon Williams	Dora Ray	14 Sep 1926
W. E. Thompson	Vessie Duke	18 Sep 1926
John McNeal	Ada B. Marr	18 Sep 1926
W. M. Waddell	Mrs. R. O. Green	20 Sep 1926
Clifton Durham	Lola Moore	18 Sep 1926
Henry Colchester	Mrs. Nellie Hard	12 Sep 1926
Lester Higginbotham	Pearl Kirkman	22 Sep 1926
Roy Fields	Eunice Bryant	22 Sep 1926
Cecil Small	Ethel Shrum	11 Sep 1926
George Keyser	Katherine Friedman	22 Sep 1926
W. M. Arnold	Ruth Hopkins	18 Sep 1026
Edward T. Howard	Mrs. Rosa Crowley	15 Sep 1926
Eulice Cobb	Nora Rogers	19 Sep 1926
R. L. Nash	Louise Finch	20 Sep 1926
J. M. Tracer	Virgie Heath	24 Sep 1926
Ernest Hicks	Lula Bell Moore	23 Sep 1926
Cokly D. Richardson	Eliza May Laster	25 Sep 1926
A. Miller	Dora Hughs	28 Sep 1926
Jim Robinson	Thelma Parker	29 Sep 1926
Arther Cook	Julia Renick	29 Sep 1926
Add Barron	Juanita Smith	30 Sep 1926
George McCarver	Mamie Trobaugh	4 Oct 1926
John McClure	Letha Haywood	4 Oct 1926
George Drazzle	Zula Groomes	22 Oct 1926
Jacob R. Jones	Mrs. Mamie Farley	30 Sep 1926
A. J. Deane	Mrs. Orphy Draper	4 Oct 1926
Charly Shdeed	Mary Hamra	3 Oct 1926
Tom Teal	Roxie D. Wallace	2 Oct 1926
Ray Cunningham	Lydie Cupp	6 Oct 1926
Sylvester Mills	Opal Stacy	4 Oct 1926

GROOM	BRIDE	SOLEMNIZED
W. E. Baugher	Alma Higgins	2 Oct 1926
B. E. Black	Merle Lee Banta	9 Oct 1926
H. A. C. Houghton	Annie Ray	6 Oct 1926
Clarence Day	Cenia Day	7 Oct 1926
W. C. Day	Eliza Sutton	7 Oct 1926
Clifford Cabaness	Lucille Williams	8 Oct 1926
V. L. Brown	Velma Stanley	6 Oct 1926
Charles Effinger	Mrs. Vader Hayes	9 Oct 1926
Delbert Rice	Mrs. Lola Boswell Dunn	10 Oct 1926
W. J. Eulitt	Mrs. Cora Wicoff	12 Oct 1926
C. Wright	Carie Wilson	9 Oct 1926
H. A. Blair	Isabelle Blair	14 Oct 1926
Ocra Dunigh	Leona Herschback	9 Oct 1926
J. Q. Montgomery	Annie Tate	16 Oct 1926
W.A. Swain	Alpha Hall	19 Oct 1926
E. O. May	Mrs. Every Walker	18 Oct 1926
W. H. Smith	Mrs. Izora Hart	18 Oct 1926
Charley Greable	Dovie Stevenson	17 Oct 1926
Orda Gibbs	Cecil Smith	17 Oct 1926
James E. Pruie	Mrs. Cole Emmerson	22 Oct 1926
Willis Rollins	Ruth Anderson	21 Oct 1926
Jim Romines	Etta Clay	17 Oct 1926
John A. Cuff	Lula Davis	16 Oct 1926
A. E. Wilson	Mrs. Lottie Cox	15 Oct 1926
W. L. Schaffer	Etta Miller	23 Oct 1926
J. W. Hicks	Cecil Sims	25 Oct 1926
J. W. C. McDonald	Florence Combs	23 Oct 1926
Clayburn Dye	Viney Austin	23 Oct 1926
Bryan Island	Pearl Moore	23 Oct 1926
Fred Mansfield	Mrs. Mamie Blankenship	23 Oct 1926
Dave Gray	August Stewart	23Ooct 1926
William Sickman	Mary Hendrix	16 Oct 1926
Donald Jackson	Pearl Dunigan	17 Oct 1926
Robert Carr	Ellen Lovins	21 Oct 1926
W. A. Turlington	Gertie Chapman	24 Oct 1926
Larkin Swope	Lillie Ross	24 Oct 1926
Leonard Hul	Myrtis Lee Coleman	30 Sep 1926
C. E. Wood	Effie Bennett	28 Oct 1926
Nute Motes	Katie Lee Whitlock	29 Oct 1926
G. C. Clark	Vera Lee Spears	30 Oct 1926
Wm. H. Holcomb	Bertie Bruce	1 Oct 1926
C. E. Williams	Lillian P. Miles	30 Oct 1926
Wallace Ford	Katie Miller	2 Nov 1926
A. T. Poe	Dollie E. Granger	3 Nov 1926

GROOM	BRIDE	SOLEMNIZED
J. F. Jackson	Mrs. Lillian M. Carter	3 Oct 1926
Dallas Stroup	Nina Belle Adams	3 Nov 1926
R. P. Cobbs	Minnie Turner	6 Nov 1926
Raymond Clark	Tracy Crossland	6 Nov 1926
Ernest Dunning	Margaret Petty	5 Nov 1926
Dewey Cope	May Huley Greenfield	8 Nov 1926
E. E. Bryant	Lillie Nugent	4 Nov 1926
Isaac C. Wilson	Mrs. M. A. Rhoads	6 Nov 1926
R. D. Walls Jr.	Ruby Fletcher	7 Nov 1926
Lester Walls	Beatrice Shrum	3 Nov 1926
Paul Yount	Lola Scott	10 Nov 1926
Hubert Smith	Mrs. Della Pane	10 Nov 1926
Bill Estes	Mrs. Carrie Pendleton	10 Nov 1926
Alonzo Fleeman	Elizabeth Osburn	9 Nov 1926
Mooring Powell	Jenny Nettleton	8 Nov 1926
Ray Douglass	Willie Cates	16 Nov 1926
L. A. Neal	Mrs. Blanche Manor	17 Nov 1926
Moreau Gaskins	Ima Nora Terry	12 Nov 1926
Sheldon J. Stratman	Emily H. Yahl	17 Nov 1926
Orville Chaney	Gladys V. Fitzgerald	15 Nov 1926
Walter Cravens	Pearl Dowdy	17 Nov 1926
R. E. Edwards	Parthena McCuen	19 Nov 1926
Bill McGrew	Eldie Dammons	18 Nov 1926
Robert Haywood	Eva Nell Osborn	20 Nov 1926
Loyd Dennison	Helen Bevins	16 Nov 1926
Loyd Goode	Oma Tracer	20 Oct 1926
Claud Williams	Margarett Jackson	21 Nov 1926
Theodore Clark Elmore	Mrs. Lydia Presley	22 Nov 1926
J. R. Hastings	Ella Malone	23 Nov 1926
J. B. Spears	Ora Clark	16 Nov 1926
J. W. Holliman	Claire E. Wilson	24 Nov 1926
Frank Gray	Bernice Skidmore	25 Nov 1926
Ira Hopkins	Essie Vivian Bowman	14 Nov 1926
Jim Lowe	Mrs. Bertie M. Thompson	25 Nov 1926
George Settlemoir	Susie Pope	21 Nov 1926
T. C. Caldwell	Mrs. Vina May Jeffrey	20 Nov 1926
Ira Killian	Elsie Deason	6 Nov 1926
Dave Shelton	Press Hyde	22 Nov 1926
Willie P. Anderson	Coner Cotton	24 Nov 1926
John Winchester	Mamie Hildebrand	29 Nov 1926
J. E. Goldsmith	Mrs. Hassie Edwards	1 Dec 1926
H. B. Spooner	Nelle Leigh	1 Dec 1926
Thos. H. Stevens	Bertha G. Imnel	16 Nov 1926
Milford Brown	Gracie Blars	17 Dec 1926

GROOM	BRIDE	SOLEMNIZED
L. G. Ingram	Mrs. Pansy Vincent	19 Dec 1926
Orville Rogers	Mabel McSpairn	15 Dec 1926
G. D. Daniels	Tempy Mabery	17 Dec 1926
Marvin King	Pearl Roberts	16 Oct 1926
Robert Holifield	Goldie Goldsmith	8 Dec 1926
L. M. Lumpkins	Lula A. Smith	9 Dec 1926
Fred Johnson	Mrs. Martha Sanders	5 Dec 1926
David Wherry	Ruby Clarks	11 Dec 1926
Isaac Day	Elsie Henson	11 Dec 1926
Mitchell Brown	Zula Mae Horton	11 Dec 1926
George Fred Henley	Willie Henley	11 Dec 1926
Ewing Prince	Esther Batson	12 Dec 1926
Jessie James	Sadie Taylor	27 Nov 1926
William Bowling	Idelle Wooten	11 Dec 1926
T. M. Jones	Mrs. Minnie Harner	11 Dec 1926
J. F. Thompson	Emma Cobb	14 Dec 1926
Troy Hudgens	Lena Landerman	14 Dec 1926
Paul E. Reymer	Agnes Bridges	20 Nov 1926
J. L. Hawkes	Georgia Carter	18 Dec 1926
Henry Tarrant	Mrs. Dorris Harner	27 Dec 1926
Fred Kirby	Josie Bever	27 Dec 1926
William Woodson	Louise Knox	25 Dec 1926
Clarence Forrest	Teadley O'Bar	26 Dec 1926
Thoedore Hollaway	Mary Gargus	26 Dec 1926
Chalmer McNew	Stella Wagner	24 Dec 1926
Thomas Russell Wilkins	Ella Mae Brannum	25 Dec 1926
Sam McClarin	Gazel Ragsdale	25 Dec 1926
Herbert McClain	Nellie Hampton	24 Dec 1926
Leroy Rodery	Sylvia Lorene Taylor	24 Dec 1926
Benson Martin	Cordie Harvey	24 Dec 1926
Walter Bridges	Mrs. Sarah Belle Crawford	21 Dec 1926
Raymond Samples	Malissa James	22 Dec 1926
Guy E. Mann	Leota Tolbert (Talbert)	18 Dec 1926
S. J. Cato	Verda Shultz	28 Dec 1926
J. C. Morris	Bertha Hobbs	28 Dec 1926
W. Harper	Allie Wineman	28 Dec 1926
James M. Halden	Mrs. Deborah Thurman	28 Dec 1926
Floyd Proffer	Alma Stanfill	29 Dec 1926
Henry Dunn	Ruth Hicks	25 Dec 1926
Pooley Lunsford	Mrs. Ada Campbell Wood	28 Oct 1926
James w. Bagwell	Mrs. Eliza Wilkins	28 Dec 1926
Louie Oto Felker	Vera Viola Wells	9 Nov 1926
George Curtis	Lizzie Hill	26 Dec 1926
Hubert Harvill	Opal Hapwood	31 Dec 1926

GROOM	BRIDE	SOLEMNIZED
Kermett Branum	Obera Swindle	1 Jan 1927
W.A. Crowe	Mabel Ellis	1 Jan 1927
R. D. Guthrie	Mrs. M. E. Williams	31 Dec 1926
George Abbott	Opal Abbott	4 Jan 1927
Herschel Yeargain	Della McPharlane	1 Jan 1927
R. D. Reynolds	Ollie McClain	5 Jan 1927
Harold Nesler	Bonnie Bishop	19 Dec 1926
W. R. Roland	Myrtie Roland	5 Jan 1927
James McCoy	Mary Moore	7 Jan 1927
Brown Robinson	Pricilla Cupper	7 Jan 1927
S. Westerfield	Lucy Warf	8 Jan 1927
William Reddick	Corena Roddy	22 Dec 1926
R. H. Timmons	Ella Pottor	24 Dec 1926
Jim Ray	Lela Kiddy	7 Jan 1927
J. B. Smith	Effie Casey	9 Jan 1927
Berlie R. Wilson	Jeffye Sloan	1 Jan 1927
Otho L. Whitaker	Esther Lambert	9 Jan 1927
J. R. Davis	May Kerney	23 Dec 1926
William B. Jones	Mrs. Elva Huffman	24 Dec 1926
A. C. Ward	Thelma Byrd	9 Jan 1927
Henry Graddy	Mabel Rundel	10 Jan 1927
E. A. Binkley	Mrs. Lona (Lora) Moore	14 Jan 1927
Raymond D. Jones	Helen Tosh	15 Jan 1927
B. L. Davenport	Mertie Taught	15 Jan 1927
T. S. McGrew	Bessie McDale	15 Jan 1927
Herman L. Lewis	Elsie Hockey	14 Jan 1927
W. F. Baker	Mrs. Georgia McCaleb	17 Jan 1927
C. Everett Brown	Bertie Parsons	17 Jan 1927
Russell Vaughn	Mrs. Iva Jordon Thompson	16 Jan 1927
Rollen Herrell	Mrs. Viona Akins	19 Jan 1927
Quary Jones	Theola Austin	8 Jan 1927
J. C. Hurt	Lettia McDaniel	24 Jan 1927
Jessie Williams	Beulah Wilburn	23 Jan 1927
J. L. Austin	Mrs. Emma McKinney	23 Jan 1927
Ray Carson	Annie Jaco	16 Jan 1927
Lee McGehee	Beulah Ray	23 Jan 1927
L. C. Tidwell	Bernice McElyea	25 Jan 1927
Louie (Lanie) Cupp	Vernia Williams	21 Jan 1927
Paul Meyer	Teresa Ronspiez (Rouspiez)	26 Jan 1927
Boss Lawson	Rzetta Morgan	29 Jan 1927
W. B. Fowler	Mrs. Mary E. Baily	31 Jan 1927
Wyman Selby	Louise Waddell	27 Jan 1927
James Langford	Lucy Steele	29 Jan 1927
Oscar Poe	Mary Renfroe	1 Feb 1927

GROOM	BRIDE	SOLEMNIZED
E. D. Smith	Clara Brooks	19 Jan 1927
Clyde Aldridge	Daisy Belle Walker	5 Feb 1927
Walter Fox	Jannie Holigan	5 Feb 1927
Ira Britton	Dovillia Landreth	5 Feb 1927
Clarence White	Mabel Johnson	6 Feb 1927
Henry A. Petty	Lola Bledsoe	9 Feb 1927
H. McCarty	Mary Eva Rushing	6 Feb 1927
Bill Patterson	Gladys Oxley	5 Feb 1927
Willie Sullivan	Alma Stokes	12 Feb 1927
M. L. Paskel	Ola Alley	11 Feb 1927
Dave Nelson	Pearl Powers	12 Feb 1927
Fred Redfern	Mrs. Ruby Caldwell	15 Feb 1927
D. S. Richardson	Mrs. Lee Webb	11 Feb 1927
Sam Raymond Cash	Lucy Bridges Medley	16 Feb 1927
Louis Wiseman	Bertha Woods	18 Feb 1927
C. A. Arthur	Lora (Lona) Hart	3 Feb 1927
Herol Glenn Nesselrodt	Mildred Irene Hammon	4 Feb 1927
J. A. Tarman	Mrs. Velma Estes	19 Feb 1927
Cecil Rogers	Marion Ellis	<u>21 Sep 1924</u>
A. L. Lacy	Mrs. Annie Swank	21 Feb 1927
Darrow McCarty	Mabel Hogan	24 Feb 1927
Truman Cable	Margaret Landsdell	10 Feb 1927
J. E. Williams	Mrs. Lucy Hubbard	27 Feb 1927
Rile Coleman	Ether Richardson	26 Feb 1927
Arthur Quinn	Venolia Montgomery	19 Feb 1927
Clayton Moore	Beady Freeman	10 Feb 1927
J. C. Stanley	M. J. Greenfield	7 Feb 1927
Jessie Miles	Melma Hamilton	5 Mar 1927
Willie Wooddard	Juanita Cooper	15 Feb 1927
Waldo F. Speer	Lena C. Frazelle	25 Feb 1927
Grover Ward	Mrs. Maggie Taylor	10 Mar 1927
Jessie Childs	Ollie Hampton	11 Mar 1927
Allen Layne	Mrs. Mary McCulley	12 Mar 1927
Clarence Eakins	Rachel Wood	12 Mar 1927
T. J. Jones	Florence Rich	12 Mar 1927
Cecil Brannum	Helen Brand (Braud)	11 Mar 1927
Emory Giles	Annie Reddick	27 Feb 1927
Arthur Rogers	Opal Armstrong	18 Mar 1927
C. L. Ragsdale	Bessie Ray	18 Mar 1927
Lester Ready	Mary Bratcher	22 Mar 1927
Arlie Hogan	Mrs. Eva McKay	22 Mar 1927
Harold Williams	Ora Mabery	18 Mar 1927
Louis Edwards	Fredia Crider	22 Mar 1927
Louie Bateman	Ethel Roach	24 Mar 1927

GROOM	BRIDE	SOLEMNIZED
W. E. Webb	Uldeen Elizabeth Stout	24 Mar 1927
Elmer Emery	Edna Rushing	20 Mar 1927
R. L. Dodson	Ollie Portwood	26 Mar 1927
L. C. Neely	Pauline Groomes	26 Mar 1927
Charlie Simpson	Mrs. Fay Abner	26 Mar 1927
Claude Howard	Edith Skidmore	26 Mar 1927
James R. Dycus	Opal Granger	13 Mar 1927
Charlie Ortes (Artes)	Josie Hampton	6 Feb 1927
J. Robinson	Elsie Wilkins	5 Apr 1927
Earl Ellege	Beulah Bailey	1 Apr 1927
Leland Faulkner	Marvordyn Roberts	22 Mar 1927
Geo. W. McGee	Mrs. Lillie Oldham	3 Apr 1927
Carl McClanahan	Mrs. Ada Joiners	6 Apr 1927
Don D. Rufus	Hattey Viola Erwin	10 Apr 1927
E. E. Richards	Ida Sturgeon	26 Mar 1927
Floyd Roberts	Stella Wilson	16 Apr 1927
Tom Jackson	Irena Lee	19 Apr 1927
Ed Mangrum	Opal Robinson	20 Apr 1927
Benjamin Coldwell Smith	Bessie Lee Moore	18 Apr 1927
Chalres Prince	Orene Jo Tomalin	17 Apr 1927
Willie Birdom	Ethel Hair	29 Mar 1927
Lloyd Jarrett	Mattie Hampton	19 Apr 1927
E. C. Mabley (Mobley)	Bessie Marie Herrell	23 Apr 1927
Oliver Dennison	Eunice Parker	30 Apr 1927
Preston Smith	Bertha Steele	30 Apr 1927
Roy Tinsley	Edith Stevens	3 May 1927
Joseph Mollineaux	Gertrude Lee	3 May 1927
James Warford	Claudine Williams	5 May 1927
Andrew Metcalf	Lottie Mary Needham	6 May 1927
Wesley Roberts	Rosie Thompson	7 May 1927

Lauten, 130
Lawson, 135, 139
Layne, 140
Leach, 129
Lee, 141
Leigh, 137
Lell, 130
Lemonds, 133
Lentz, 129
Lewis, 130-131, 139
Liggett, 131
Lovelace, 133
Lovins, 136
Lowe, 137
Loyd, 130
Luallen, 132
Luker, 135
Lumpkins, 138
Lunsford, 138
Lutes, 132
Mabery, 138, 140
Mabley, 141
Malone, 131, 133, 137
Maness, 129
Mangrum, 141
Mann, 138
Manor, 137
Mansfield, 136
Mapel, 135
Marr, 135
Marshall, 132
Martin, 133, 138
Masters, 132
Masterson, 130
Mattingly, 135
May, 136
Mayberry, 131
McCaleb, 139
McCallum, 133
McCarty, 131, 140
McCarver, 135
McClain, 129, 138-139
McClanahan, 141
McClarin, 138

McClure, 136
McCombs, 130
McCormick, 134
McCoy, 139
McCuen, 137
McCullough, 134
McCulley, 140
McDale, 139
McDaniel, 139
McDonald, 136
McElyea, 139
McGahey, 131
McGee, 141
McGehee, 139
McGrew 137, 139
McKabee, 129
McKay, 140
McKenzie, 130
McKinney, 139
McLain, 134
McLean, 134
McMurphy, 134
McNeal, 135
McNew, 138
McPharlane, 139
McPherson, 131
McRoy, 132
McSpairn, 138
Meadows, 135
Medley, 140
Medling, 135
Meely, 133
Melton, 133
Merideth, 134
Merrick, 131
Metcalf, 141
Mewson, 133
Meyer, 139
Meyers, 129
Milburn, 131
Miles, 136, 140
Miller, 130, 133, 135-136
Mills, 129, 132, 135
Minor, 134
Minton, 131

Mitchell, 130
Mizell, 131
Mobley, 135, 141
Mollineaux, 141
Montgomery, 133, 136, 140
Moore, 129, 131, 135-136, 139-141
Morgan, 139
Morris, 129-130, 132, 134, 138
Motes, 136
Mullikin, 133
Murphy, 132
Murray, 131
Nash, 135
Neal, 137
Needham, 141
Neely, 129, 141
Neill, 134
Nelson, 140
Nesler, 139
Nesselrodt, 140
Nettleton, 137
Nolen, 132
Nuckolls, 131
Nugent, 137
O'Bar, 138
O'Dell, 132
Oakes, 133
Oldham, 135, 141
Olds, 132
Oliver, 129, 134
Ortes, 141
Osborn, 137
Osburn, 137
Ownby, 133
Oxley, 140
Pane, 137
Parish, 133-134
Parker, 133-135, 141
Parsons, 139
Paskel, 140
Patrick, 133
Patterson, 130, 134, 140

146

Printed in the United States
51550LVS00001BA/159-172